MOTORBOOKS COLORTECH

LOCKHEED SECRET PROJECTS
INSIDE THE SKUNK WORKS

DENNIS R. JENKINS

MBI Publishing Company

Acknowledgments

I would like to extend my deep gratitude to Denny Lombard at Skunk Works for finding most of the photos shown in this book. The ones not supplied by Denny were mostly supplied by Tony Landis from his outstanding collection. In addition I would like to thank Gary Griggs at Skunk Works, and Mike Moore at LMTAS for their encouragement and support. I would also like to thank several current and former Skunk Works employees who graciously shared stories with me, but wish to remain anonymous. For those interested in a more in-depth review of the early projects discussed in this book, I highly recommend picking up a copy of *Skunk Works: The Official History* by my good friend, Jay Miller.

First published in 2001 by MBI Publishing Company, Galtier Plaza, Suite 200, 380 Jackson Street, St. Paul, MN 55101-3885 USA

© Dennis R. Jenkins, 2001

The information in this book is true and complete to the best of our knowledge. All recommendations are made without any guarantee on the part of the author or Publisher, who also disclaim any liability incurred in connection with the use of this data or specific details.

We recognize that some words, model names and designations, for example, mentioned herein are the property of the trademark holder. We use them for identification purposes only. This is not an official publication.

MBI Publishing Company books are also available at discounts in bulk quantity for industrial or sales-promotional use. For details write to Special Sales Manager at Motorbooks International Wholesalers & Distributors, Galtier Plaza, Suite 200, 380 Jackson Street, St. Paul, MN 55101-3885 USA.

Library of Congress Cataloging-in-Publication Data
Jenkins, Dennis R.
    Lockheed Secret Projects : inside the Skunk Works / Dennis R. Jenkins.
        p. cm. — (ColorTech)
    Includes index.
    ISBN 0-7603-0914-0 (pbk. : alk. paper)
    1. Lockheed airplanes—History. 2. Lockheed Advanced Development Company—History.
3. Aeronautics—Research—United States—History.
4. Aeronautics, Military—Research—United States—History. 5. Research aircraft—United States—History. I. Title. II. MBI Publishing Company ColorTech.

TL686.L6 J45 2001
629.13'007'2073—dc21   2001030747

Edited by Amy Glaser
Designed by Katie Sonmor

Printed in China

Contents

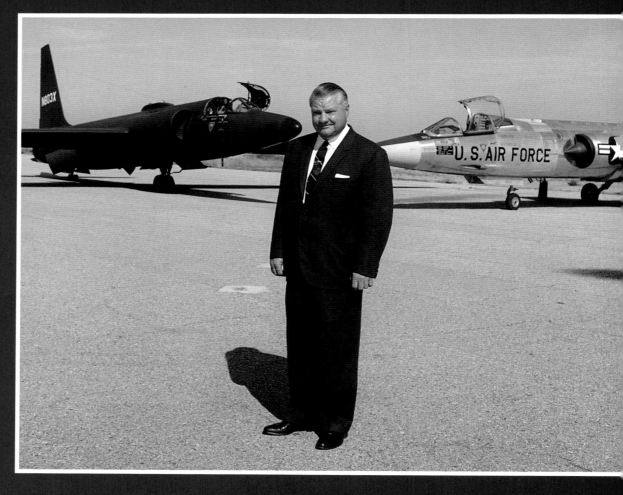

Kelly Johnson poses with two of his most famous creations, the U-2 (left) and F-104. Johnson joined Lockheed on August 21, 1933, as its 36th employee and made $83 a month. Johnson officially retired in 1975, but was retained by the company as a senior advisor until his death on December 21, 1990. During his tenure at Lockheed, Johnson won about every medal and commendation one can imagine, including the Medal of Freedom, the Nation's top civilian award, in 1964. *Lockheed Martin Skunk Works*

>>> Preface

During the last half of the twentieth century, Lockheed Skunk Works built a rather unique reputation. Almost routinely, this elite group developed landmark aircraft that redefined the possibilities of flight, although in many cases it was years after the aircraft were created that the public found out about them. Skunk Works is largely identified with a single individual—Clarence L. "Kelly" Johnson, although four others have headed the organization since Johnson's retirement.

The Skunk Works philosophy, long before it became a company, was first employed to develop the XP-80 Shooting Star, America's first production jet aircraft. Since then, Skunk Works has created aviation icons such as the F-104 Starfighter, U-2, SR-71 Blackbird, F-117A stealth fighter, and will soon introduce the X-33 and VentureStar.™

The Skunk Works name can be traced back to the "Skonk Works" brewery of Al Capp's popular *Lil' Abner* comic strip. This comic was a favorite of the Lockheed engineers during the 1940s, and Irving Culver, the engineer in charge of the XP-80's fuselage design, is widely credited for lending the name to Johnson's organization. When interviewed in 1993 by Richard Abrams, Culver recalled that security restrictions prohibited anybody on the XP-80 project from revealing their location or function when answering the phone. The resulting isolation reminded Culver of the Skonk Works in Capp's comic strip.

One day, during mid-1943, navy officials in Washington were trying to call Lockheed's Dick Pulver and were mistakenly put through to Culver's desk. When the phone rang, Culver answered it with "Skonk Works, inside man Culver." After an awkward pause, one of the navy officers asked, "What?" Culver repeated, "Skonk Works." The name stuck.

Culver remembers Johnson was not altogether pleased with the situation. Culver said that when Johnson first heard about the incident "he told me I was fired. Of course, he fired me about twice a day anyway." Eventually, Johnson warmed up to the name.

During the 1960s, as Skonk Works became known to the general public, Al Capp objected to the name, so the spelling was changed to Skunk Works, and the familiar skunk logo soon followed. In 1973, Lockheed trademarked the name and the skunk logo. As an actual entity, Skunk Works did not exist before 1953 or 1954. Most of the projects prior to this time were conducted in either the Preliminary Design Department, or by small spin-off groups set up for a specific project. When the operation became "official," it was called the Advanced Development Projects Division of the Lockheed-California Company. It was later broken out as the Lockheed Advanced Development Company (LADC). During most of this period Skunk Works was based in Burbank, California, although actual manufacturing was usually performed elsewhere. On December 22, 1992, LADC moved to the vacant L-1011 production facility (Site 10) at Air Force Plant 42 in Palmdale, California, and consolidated most operations in a single location.

When Lockheed and Martin Marietta merged in 1995, the LADC became the Lockheed Martin Skunk Works and a separate company within the new corporation. This marked the first official use of the Skunk Works name, albeit briefly. Financial considerations in early 2000 resulted in Lockheed Martin combining its three aircraft design and manufacturing operations—Fort Worth, Marietta, and Palmdale—into a single company headquartered in Fort Worth. Officially, Skunk Works ceased to exist, becoming instead the Palmdale Operations Division of Lockheed Martin Aeronautics Company.

One

The XF-90 looked remarkably advanced for its time here with Tony LeVier standing in the cockpit. Note the covers over the gun holes under the intake—production aircraft would have carried six 20-mm cannons. At various times Lockheed had investigated arming the XF-90 with rotary rocket pods under the fuselage and wingtip pods that could house fuel and missiles much like the F-89 Scorpion. *Tony Landis Collection*

>> Before Skunk Works—
SHOOTING STARS TO STARFIGHTERS

Clarence Leonard Johnson was the seventh of nine children born to Peter and Christine Johnson. If anybody, even an airplane person, is going to be able to name a contemporary aircraft designer, it is likely to be "Kelly" Johnson. In an age of increasingly anonymous corporate faces, Johnson managed to stand out among his peers and become a legend in the process.

The corporation behind Johnson, of course, was Lockheed. Founded by two brothers, Malcolm and Allan Loughead, its history can be traced to the Alco Hydro-Aeroplane Company of 1912. Alco failed in 1913, but Allan and Malcolm teamed up again in 1916 to develop the Model G biplane and formed the Loughead Aircraft Manufacturing Company. The company failed in 1921. During 1926 Allan convinced a group of bankers to start a company again, and tired of the constant mispronunciations, changed the company's spelling to the phonetic "Lockheed." With the assistance of the visionary engineer John K. "Jack" Northrop, Allan Loughead built a solid reputation for the new Lockheed Aircraft Company, and by 1928 had 50 employees at his Burbank factory.

In the late 1920s, the aircraft industry was much like the communications and computer industry is now.

Consolidations, mergers, and stock swaps were commonplace, and during mid-1929, a buyout offer was presented to the Lockheed board of directors. Much to the chagrin of Allan Loughead, the board accepted, and the four months prior to the stock market crash of 1929 were spent operating as a subsidiary of the Detroit Aircraft Corporation. Allan Loughead left the company and stayed away until 1969 when he came back to be a part-time consultant.

Neither the departure of Jack Northrop in March 1928 to form his own company, nor of Loughead in 1929, nor the Great Depression had a serious effect on Lockheed. Gerald Vultee was hired to replace Northrop, and construction of Vega, Air Express, Sirius, Orion, and Altair aircraft continued to be profitable, but ultimately proved insufficient to offset the losses of the parent corporation. On October 27, 1931, Detroit Aircraft Corporation declared bankruptcy. The Lockheed subsidiary soldiered on for a while, but it finally discontinued operations on June 16, 1932.

The company known today as Lockheed truly came into being when Robert Gross bought the assets of the Lockheed subsidiary from the bankruptcy court in late

During Lockheed's early years, the resident engineering genius was Hall Hibbard, shown here with a model of the L-133 jet fighter concept. Hibbard was a graduate of the Massachusetts Institute of Technology. *Lockheed Martin Skunk Works*

1932. It was a wise $40,000 investment. Gross hired Lloyd Stearman as general manager who, along with chief engineer Robert von Hake and assistant chief engineer Hall Hibbard, set about designing a modern twin-engine, all-metal monoplane transport—the Model 10 Electra.

Lockheed Meets Johnson

In 1932, Kelly Johnson graduated from the University of Michigan with a bachelor's degree in aeronautical engineering, and applied for an engineering job with Lockheed the following year. He was not turned down; but he was not accepted either. Instead, von Hake suggested Johnson return to the University of Michigan and complete his master's degree in aeronautical engineering.

Johnson made the best of his time at Michigan. Along with his best friend, Don Palmer, Johnson rented the university wind tunnel and conducted independent tests for anybody willing to pay. The Studebaker Motor Company commissioned Johnson and Palmer to run drag tests on the Pierce Silver Arrow, and the pair quickly discovered that the big exposed headlights on the soon-to-be-classic car were eating up 16 percent of the horsepower at 65 miles per hour. Their recommendations caused Studebaker to fair the headlights into the fenders, starting an automotive design trend. While at Michigan,

Johnson and Palmer also participated in the wind tunnel testing of the Lockheed Model 10 and were very surprised by its marginal stability in some flight regimes. This instability was an accepted condition in aircraft of the period, but Johnson was sure it could be cured.

A year later, with a master's degree in hand, Johnson showed up at the Burbank offices of a newly rejuvenated Lockheed looking for employment. On August 21, 1933,

A quiet residential area of Burbank, California, or is it? This was the Lockheed plant during World War II, covered by camouflage netting to disguise it from possible Japanese bombers. A few small aircraft can be seen at the bottom edge next to the buildings. The view under the netting shows how it was suspended on large wooden poles over the parking lot. *Lockheed Martin Skunk Works*

company's flagship product, the Model 10. Rather unceremoniously, Johnson told the meeting that the Model 10 was grossly unstable and that he felt that a better and safer aircraft could be designed. Needless to say, this did not go over well with the senior engineering staff in the room, especially coming from a recent college graduate. Instead of simply firing him, Hibbard sent Johnson back to the University of Michigan wind tunnel to prove his point. Seventy-three wind tunnel runs later, Johnson had refined the Model 10 into a much better handling aircraft. Removing the wing-root filets helped stabilize the aircraft, but the breakthrough was the addition of vertical endplates on the horizontal stabilizer. Further investigation led to the endplates becoming full-fledged vertical stabilizers, and the removal of the original single vertical stabilizer above the fuselage. Johnson returned to Burbank as something of a hero and a legend in the making. Perhaps what was more important to Johnson was that he was now regarded as a contributing member of the engineering staff.

With the improved stability of the Model 10, Johnson had given birth to the product line, including the eventual Model 14, that would provide Lockheed's initial financial success. In these early years Johnson would also be somewhat involved in the creation of the Model 22, which became the P-38 Lightning, and several other projects. This was only a preview of Johnson's ability, and his ultimate success would come much later.

In 1937 Johnson married a young paymaster at Lockheed, Althea Louis Young. The following year he was named the chief research engineer for Lockheed,

he became the 36th employee of the company and accepted a position as a tool designer for $83 per month. Don Palmer also came West and was hired by the Vultee Airplane Company in nearby Glendale.

It was almost a very short tenure in Burbank for Johnson. Within a few days of arriving, he found himself in a meeting with Cyril Chappellet (a major shareholder in the company) and Hall Hibbard to discuss the

Kelly Johnson holds a model of the L-133 while standing in front of a drawing of the ASTOVL concept that would eventually be rolled into the Joint Strike Fighter effort. Both aircraft used forward canards, and were more advanced than any of their contemporaries, but neither would be built. *Tony Landis Collection*

The XP-80 (44-83020) before its first flight. Note the high polish on the exterior surface and the winged-star Lockheed logo on the nose and vertical stabilizer. The only other exterior markings were national insignias on each side of the fuselage and top and bottom of the wings. The upper surface was a very dark blue-green with medium gray undersides. *Lockheed Martin Skunk Works*

and was also allowed to hire some of the engineers who would help him in the years to come: Willis Hawkins and Carl Haddon from the University of Michigan, and Irv Culver from CalTech. Don Palmer would come to Lockheed from Vultee within a year or two.

In the meantime, similar to most other aircraft manufacturers of the era, Lockheed suffered turbulent times. In early 1938 the company's future looked bleak. Orders were down and no major prospects were on the horizon. A contract from the British government on June 23, 1938, for more than 200 Hudson bombers (based on the Model 14) ended the slump. Lockheed was again financially viable, and would remain so for the next 30 years.

The next surge of prosperity for Lockheed occurred in the early 1940s. World War II was good to the entire American aviation industry, and Lockheed was no exception. In addition to building its own aircraft, notably the P-38 and Model 14, Lockheed also license-built the Boeing-designed B-17 Flying Fortress. Between July 1, 1940, and August 31, 1945, Lockheed built

The second XP-80A (44-83022) was usually called *Silver Ghost* since it lacked the gloss gray paint of the first aircraft. As shown here the aircraft was modified to test the afterburning Westinghouse J34 turbojet that was planned for the XF-90 program. Note how the silver finish changes hue just aft of the national insignia, showing where the fuselage has been modified to accept the larger engine and afterburner. *Tony Landis Collection*

The P-80 established a precedent: Skunk Works would design and flight-test an aircraft, and then turn production over to the mainstream Lockheed organizations that were better equipped to accomplish it. Here a very early P-80 assembly line is shown co-located with the P-38 Lightning production line Although still largely a novelty at this point, jet-powered fighters would soon make even the best of the piston-engine aircraft obsolete. *Lockheed Martin Skunk Works*

19,077 aircraft and was the fifth largest aircraft manufacturer in the United States.

The road to Skunk Works began just prior to World War II, and for 15 years the people involved kept alive a concept of how aircraft should be designed and programs should be managed. During these years Skunk Works existed only in the minds of those involved. Officially most of the projects were conducted under the auspices of the Preliminary Design Department, although occasionally a large project would be spun off into its own group for a short while. A short description of some of the more significant projects, usually ones that made it to the prototype stage or further, follows.

The L-133

During the early 1940s, having essentially nothing to do with what became Skunk Works, Hibbard and Johnson, along with Phil Colman, Willis Hawkins, and the forward-thinking Nathan Price, quietly explored what they believed the next generation

The lone XP-80R was modified from the XP-80B proto-type (48-5200) in an attempt to set a world speed record. Initially the aircraft was fitted with a pair of ungainly looking NACA-duct air intakes, but these soon gave way to the more conventional intakes seen here. A special version of the J33 engine, called the Allison Model 400, used water-methanol injection to produce 4,600 pounds-force. This aircraft has a smaller, streamlined canopy and highly polished paint. On June 19, 1947, this aircraft managed an average 623.8 miles per hour, and gave the United States its first world speed record in over 20 years. *Lockheed Martin Skunk Works*

of combat aircraft would look like. The outcome was the L-133—a jet-propelled aircraft that used a rear-mounted straight main wing along with a forward canard. A pair of Lockheed-developed 5,500-pounds-thrust L-1000 axial-flow turbojets would have to provide a maximum speed of 600 miles per hour. It looks advanced, even 60 years later. On February 24, 1942, Lockheed submitted a report on the L-133 to the army at Wright Field. The expediencies of war and the need to rapidly produce existing combat aircraft, however, left precious few resources to pursue such an advanced concept, and no further action was taken on it.

By late 1944, it was obvious that the Allies would be victorious. There were still many bloody battles to be won, but momentum was irrevocably on the side of the United States. The military began to allow aircraft companies to divert some resources from the production of combat aircraft to advanced studies. Around this time Lockheed transferred the design and technology for the L-1000 to Menasco, which subsequently built and tested several major components, but never assembled a complete engine. It did not really matter since by now the L-1000 engine had been largely overshadowed by the technologically inferior deHavilland H.1B Goblin centrifugal-flow turbojet.

During 1947 Lockheed modified two P-80As to test various Marquardt ramjets. The aircraft were fitted with stronger horizontal and vertical stabilizers, and the wingtips were modified to accept 20-, 30-, or 48-inch-diameter ramjets, although it appears the 48-inch units were never actually installed. A small second seat for an observer was installed in lieu of the normal fuselage fuel tank immediately behind the pilot. Testing continued through 1948 and showed that the engines could be operated successfully. Similar tests, at much higher speeds, would be conducted in the future using the Lockheed X-7. *Lockheed Martin Skunk Works*

By using a 29-inch fuselage plug ahead of the wing and a 12-inch plug aft, Don Palmer and his team managed to stuff a fully configured second seat into the P-80 and created the T-33 jet trainer. This also became the first of the new jet fighters to use ejection seats, and a Lockheed-designed unit was provided for both pilots. The T-33 would long outlive its single-seat counterpart, and even today it is not uncommon to see a T-33 flying, although none remain in active U.S. military service. In an odd twist of fate, Boeing is using a specially configured T-33 as an "adversary" during the development of the avionics for its Joint Strike Fighter. *Lockheed Martin Skunk Works*

Developing a Legend—Be Quick, Be Quiet, Be on Time

The experience gained while investigating the L-133 put Lockheed in a unique position during 1943 when the Army Air Forces asked the company to investigate a jet-powered fighter based on the British Goblin engine. As unproductive as the L-133 project had seemed at the time—no real hardware was built and no aircraft was flown—the experience provided the beginnings of Lockheed's, and Johnson's, rise to fame.

Because of Johnson's stated interest in jet propulsion, Robert Gross assigned the young engineer to develop Lockheed's response to the army's request. Johnson was eager for the opportunity, but wanted to do things his own way. Johnson said in his autobiography: "For some time I had been pestering Gross and Hibbard

to let me set up an experimental department where the designers and shop artisans could work together closely in development of airplanes without the delays and complications of intermediate departments to handle administration, purchasing, and all the other support functions. I wanted a direct relationship between design engineer and mechanic and manufacturing. I decided to handle this new project just that way."

Within a month of the initial request, the team led by Johnson had assembled a preliminary design for the L-140, and the data package was personally delivered by Johnson to Wright Field on June 15, 1943. Two days later the army approved the concept, and on June 23, the army issued a letter contract that allowed Johnson to begin work. By October 16, a $642,404 contract had been signed for project MX-604—the XP-80. The contractual aspects were immaterial. Unbelievably, Johnson had

The little Model 75 Saturn gave a fairly accurate look at the future of small transports. The high-wing design allowed the fuselage to sit low to the ramp, and made moving people and material on and off much easier. This same basic philosophy would be used when it came time to design the C-130 Hercules, and also carried through to the jet-powered C-141 and C-5 transports. In the end, however, there were simply too many surplus wartime transports on the market that could be purchased for a fraction of the cost of a new Saturn and the program was cancelled. *Lockheed Martin Skunk Works*

agreed to provide the first aircraft 150 days after the letter contract had been signed. Kelly Johnson, along with Art Viereck and Don Palmer, began setting up the new department. Johnson and Palmer had been best friends at the University of Michigan, and Palmer drew up the principles upon which the XP-80 prototype effort would be guided. Over the next 10 years, these principles became Skunk Work's operating rules, although they are usually, and incorrectly, attributed to Johnson himself.

The rules were important to the ultimate success of the XP-80. For instance, the Drawing Room Manual for the L-140 project stated: "Any type of drawing may be

used provided it contains sufficient information to build the part or assembly." If the project had been burdened by a complex drawing system or any overly complicated rules, there is no way the aircraft could have been completed in 150 days.

The Burbank plant was filled to capacity with wartime production projects, and because of the secrecy surrounding the jet engine, the XP-80 team was removed from the normal work areas. Johnson and his team took over an area in the Burbank facility that had been used as a wind tunnel model construction area. The first order of business was to construct a partial mockup based on the preliminary design presented to the Army; wind tunnel runs were the next step.

As the project continued, the team quickly grew, and by midsummer there were about 25 engineers and 100 shop mechanics working on the XP-80. A temporary lean-to with walls salvaged from wooden shipping crates and a canvas roof was built adjacent to the wind tunnel building to house the overflow of workers. The lean-to was poorly lit, extremely cramped, and until the end of July, not air-conditioned. Given the over-100-degree-Fahrenheit-days in Burbank at that time of the year, the conditions could not have been conducive to developing the first production American jet fighter.

Nevertheless, work progressed at a rapid pace. By August 12, Johnson noted that engineering for the prototype was "68.7 percent complete." On September 11, the final assembly began except for one minor detail: Lockheed did not have a Goblin engine. A working, but nonflyable, engine finally arrived from England on November 3, to clear the way for finishing the first XP-80. The next 10 days were spent completing a myriad of details, and finally, on November 13, the XP-80 was completed 140 days after the project had begun. The aircraft was immediately disassembled and loaded on a trailer for an overland trip to Muroc Army Air Field in the Mojave Desert, known today as Edwards Air Force Base. In the meantime, a flyable engine arrived. The Goblin engine in the XP-80 was started for the first time on

November 17, 1943, but the engine was subsequently damaged and deemed unflyable. A new engine arrived at Muroc on December 28, and was installed in the XP-80 the following day. Lockheed chief test pilot Milo Burcham took the XP-80 for its maiden flight on January 8, 1944, in front of an audience including Robert Gross, Cyril Chappellet, various army officials, and 140 members of the team that had built it. This would become another tradition: as many of the team as possible were always invited for first flights.

The first flight of the XP-80 uncovered various minor anomalies, but these were quickly corrected and a second flight was conducted later in the afternoon. The aircraft was docile, fast, and maneuverable, and the Army Air Forces was impressed. By the end of March the aircraft had attained 506 miles per hour at 20,000 feet, and became the first American aircraft to exceed 500 miles per hour in level flight. Ultimately the XP-80 would be used as a testbed and trainer until June 10, 1946, when it was officially retired. It was sent to the Smithsonian in 1949, and a complete restoration of the airframe was accomplished during 1979.

During the weeks Johnson had been waiting for the second engine to arrive from England, he had given approval for the team at Burbank to begin work on the L-141 that was designated XP-80A by the Army. This aircraft would incorporate many of the lessons that were learned from building the first XP-80, and would be much more representative of future production models. As with the XP-80, Johnson had promised the army that the two XP-80As would be completed within a short time period, in this case 120 days. It was 138 days before well-known P-38 test pilot Tony LeVier took the first XP-80A on its maiden flight.

The L-141 represented a further definition of the philosophy that would become part of Skunk Works tradition. A small group outside the bounds of the normal Lockheed bureaucracy would be used to design and build the prototypes. If and when a follow-on production contract was issued, a cadre of the engineers and craftsmen would follow the project back into the mainstream Lockheed organization to ensure a smooth transition into production.

There was one other P-80 assignment given to Johnson's team before they all moved on to other projects. On November 11, 1945, a Royal Air Force Gloster Meteor Mk.4 set a new world speed record of 606.25 miles per hour. The Army Air Forces and Lockheed concluded that a modified P-80 could break this record, and Gen. Henry H. (Hap) Arnold authorized spending $75,000 on the attempt. Two P-80As would ultimately be used. One was slightly modified and equipped with a

An unusual failure for Skunk Works was the Model 89 Constitution. It was a remarkably large aircraft for its time, and Lockheed had to build a new six-story facility at Burbank just to assemble the two prototypes. The cancellation of the turboprop engine that was supposed to power the aircraft ensured that it would be significantly underpowered, although the two that were completed served several useful years in Navy service. *Lockheed Martin Skunk Works*

The Skunk Works Operating Rules

Kelly Johnson continually refined the basic rules established by Don Palmer during the development of the XP-80. The 14 rules would seem to be common sense, but often the rules flew in the face of standard military and aerospace industry practice. Interestingly, as Skunk Works grew and became more bureaucratic, the industry as a whole was trying to reverse the trend and become more streamlined and efficient. Finally, during the 1990s, the military canceled many of the "mil-specs" and other procedures that had long hindered commercial entities, and told the industry to adopt the "best commercial practices"—what Kelly Johnson had been advocating for 40 years. The parenthetical comments explain some of the rationale for the rules.

1. The Skunk Works manager must be delegated practically complete control of his program in all aspects. He should report to a division president or higher. (*It is essential that the program manager have authority to make decisions quickly regarding technical, finance, schedule, or operations matters.*)

2. Strong, but small, project offices must be provided by both the customer and contractor. (*The customer program manager must have similar authority to that of the contractor.*)

3. The number of people having any connection with the project must be restricted in an almost vicious manner. Use of a small number of good people. (*Bureaucracy makes unnecessary work and must be brutally controlled.*)

4. A very simple drawing and drawing release system with great flexibility for making changes must be provided. (*This permits early work by manufacturing organizations, and schedule recovery if technical risks involve failures.*)

5. There must be a minimum of reports required, but important work must be recorded thoroughly. (*Responsible management does not require massive technical and information systems.*)

6. There must be a monthly cost review covering not only what has been spent and committed, but also projected costs to the conclusion of the program. Don't have the books 90 days late and don't surprise the customer with sudden overruns. (*Responsible management does require operation within the resources available.*)

7. The contractor must be delegated and must assume more than normal responsibility to get good vendor bids for the subcontract on the project. Commercial bid procedures are very often

better than military ones. (*Essential freedom to use the best talent available and operate within the resources available.*)

8. The inspection system as currently used by the Skunk Works, which has been approved by both the Air Force and Navy, meets the intent of existing military requirements and should be used on new projects. Push more basic inspection responsibility back to the subcontractors and vendors. Don't duplicate so much inspection. (*Even the commercial world recognizes that quality is in design and responsible organizations; not inspection.*)

9. The contractor must be delegated the authority to test his final product in flight. He can and must test it in the initial stages. If he doesn't, he rapidly loses his competency to design other vehicles. (*Critical if new technology and the attendant risks are to be rationally accommodated.*)

10. The specification applying to the hardware must be agreed to in advance of contracting. The Skunk Works practice of having a specification section stating clearly which important military specification items will not knowingly be complied with and reasons therefore is highly recommended. (*Standard specifications inhibit new technology and innovation, and are frequently obsolete.*)

11. Funding a program must be timely so that the contractor doesn't have to keep running to the bank to support government projects. (*Rational management requires knowledge of, and freedom to use, the resources originally committed.*)

12. There must be mutual trust between the customer project organization and the contractor with very close cooperation and liaison on a day-to-day basis. This cuts down misunderstanding and correspondence to an absolute minimum. (*The goals of the customer and producer should be the same—to get the job done well.*)

13. Access by outsiders to the project and its personnel must be strictly controlled by appropriate security measures. (*This is a program manager's responsibility even if no security demands are made; a cost avoidance measure.*)

14. Because only a few people will be used in engineering and most other areas, ways must be provided to reward good performance by pay not based on the number of personnel supervised. (*Responsible management must be rewarded, and responsible management does not permit the growth of bureaucracies.*)

Although it was a disappointing performer, the XF-90 (note the nose says F-90) pioneered the use of 75ST aluminum, a stronger alloy that would eventually become common on high-performance aircraft. The primary reason for the XF-90's lack of performance was that the pair of 3,000-pounds-thrust Westinghouse XJ34-WE-11 engines initially used were underpowered. Even the addition of afterburners (creating 4,200-pounds-thrust XJ-34-WE-15s) did little to help overall performance, although at least the aircraft could now get off the ground without the use of rocket-assisted take-off (RATO) bottles. *Tony Landis Collection*

water-injected Allison J33 engine; the other would be extensively modified into the XP-80R. After some initial disappointments, on June 19, 1947, the XP-80R managed to fly at 623.8 miles per hour, giving the United States its first official world speed record in almost a quarter-century.

With the completion of the two XP-80As and the speed record aircraft, the P-80 program moved totally within the mainstream Lockheed organization. The P-80, named "Shooting Star" by Gross and Hibbard, would go on to a long and successful career in the service of at least half a dozen air forces. It would also lay claim to the first all-jet aerial combat victory when an F-80C flown by Lt. Russell Brown shot down a MiG 15 over Korea on November 7, 1950. Eventually, a total of 1,732 P-80s were manufactured, and some remained in service with the U.S. Air Force as late as 1958.

A Two-Seater

A version of the P-80 would come back to Skunk Works. By 1947 it was obvious that the typical air force combat pilot was having a hard time adjusting to the

new jet aircraft. Although pilots were given extensive ground schooling, their first flight experience in a jet was always solo since there were no existing two-seat jet fighters. In early 1947 Gross committed $1 million of Lockheed funds to design, manufacture, and test a two-seat variant of the P-80. Gross figured his investment would be paid back when the air force ordered the new variant into production.

Don Palmer was slated to lead the team that would take an uncompleted P-80C off the production line and modify it into a two-seat trainer. Palmer conducted the modifications in typical Skunk Works fashion—surrounded by almost total secrecy. In this case it was not so much to hide the new aircraft from the Soviets, but from competing manufacturers who might decide to make two-seat variants of the Republic F-84 or North American F-86. Tony LeVier took the first TP-80C on its maiden flight on March 22, 1948, and it was soon discovered that the slightly longer aircraft performed marginally better than its single-seat counterpart.

Two weeks later, the Air Force ordered 20 production TP-80Cs, although the designation was officially changed to T-33A on June 11, 1948. The Navy was sufficiently impressed to order 26 similar TO-2s (the Navy version of the T-33A). Like the P-80 before it, production of the T-33 was handled by the mainstream Lockheed factory, and Don Palmer and the others quietly began work on other projects. Eventually, Lockheed manufactured 5,691 T-33s of various models, an additional 656 were built by Canadair in Canada, and 210 were manufactured by Kawasaki in Japan. The aircraft would serve with more than two dozen air forces around the world, and some are still operating today. The investment Gross put into the development of this project was a good decision on his part.

The Fast Action Shop

Contrary to popular belief, Skunk Works has not always concentrated on highly classified military projects. Part of the problem lies in the fact that Skunk Works, as an identifiable entity, did not exist prior to 1954. The prototype team led by Johnson was disbanded after the P-80 was turned over to the mainstream Lockheed organization, but various members of that team subsequently contributed to other projects within Lockheed. Each member of the team remembered the lessons they had learned while building the XP-80s and applied some of these lessons to other projects, but there was little that could be pointed to as the "Skunk Works," and this makes tracing its history difficult.

In the nine years between handing off the P-80 production and the beginning of the U-2 project, various former members of the XP-80 prototype team participated in at least 10 major engineering projects for the Lockheed-California Company. None of these projects would be created in a true Skunk Works atmosphere, but all would use various aspects of the rapid-prototyping approach that had been pioneered by Johnson and Palmer. Several of the projects would ultimately produce aircraft that are world famous, and one remains in production to this day, but the remaining projects have been forgotten and are only obscure footnotes in aviation history.

A line of F-94Bs undergoing final checks at Palmdale prior to delivery. The T-33 heritage is obvious except for the revised rear fuselage that housed an afterburning 6,000-pounds-force J33-A-33 engine. The radar for the E-1 fire control system was housed behind the white radome on the upper nose. Tony LeVier took the prototype YF-94B on its maiden flight on September 29, 1950, and found few differences from the proceeding F-94A series. *Lockheed Martin Skunk Works*

The Model 75 Saturn

The first of these projects predates the XP-80 project in many respects. Toward the end of World War II, Lockheed began planning the transport aircraft it expected to build for the postwar civilian market. An extensive market survey indicated two types of aircraft would be required. The first could be satisfied with an updated version of the graceful Model 1049 Constellation airliner that had first been produced as the Army C-69 in 1943. The second would be a smaller aircraft designed, according to Lockheed, "to do the big business of the little airline and the little business of the big airline."

The resulting aircraft, the L-146, was designed under the direction of Don Palmer and Willis Hawkins more or less concurrently with the development of the XP-80. The first opportunity to market the new design came at the Chicago International Air Conference held in August 1944. Lockheed promoted the new aircraft, named Saturn, and soon received tentative orders for more than 500 aircraft. The high priority assigned to the XP-80 slowed work on the Saturn, and it was not until the middle of 1945 that construction of the first of two prototypes began.

The Model 75 Saturn (Lockheed uses L-numbers for design studies, and a different model series for production programs) was among the first transport to make use of the advances in technology that were developed during the war, such as the laminar flow wing. It was designed to carry 14 passengers from unimproved airfields, could be quickly converted to an all-cargo configuration capable of carrying 3,000 pounds, or could accommodate any combination of cargo and passengers. Palmer and his team had optimized the aircraft to need little ground support equipment. The fuselage was set very low to allow passengers to step directly into it, or for trucks to back up to the door and easily offload cargo. The main landing gear doors, engines, cowlings, and control surfaces were interchangeable from left to right, and eliminated the need for small airlines to maintain a large quantity of spare parts. It was a well-thought-out design that was years ahead of most aircraft in terms of easy maintenance.

Despite the promotional markings, this aircraft was not one of the YF-94C prototypes. The F-94C was the ultimate development of the original P-80, and a surprisingly large amount of the basic design can still be seen. The production F-94Cs introduced a completely revised nose that housed an array of unguided rockets around the center-mounted AN/APG-40 radar. *Lockheed Martin Skunk Works*

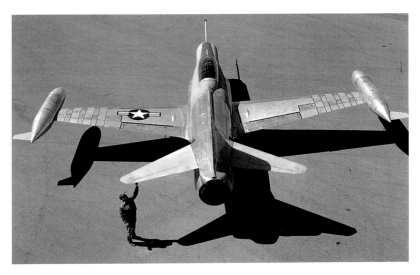

The first YF-94C had been built by Lockheed as a private venture and initially carried the civil registration N34C. Later in its career, it was assigned the Air Force serial number 50-955 and was painted with these unique orange markings, which forced the national insignia on top of the wing further inboard than normal. One of the most visible differences between the F-94C and previous models was the swept horizontal stabilizer. *Lockheed Martin Skunk Works*

The X-7 was a relatively small vehicle, which was a necessity considering it was carried under the wing of a Boeing B-29. A Marquardt ramjet (probably a 28-inch-diameter engine) can be seen under the fuselage. The ramjet tests were conducted to aid the development of the Boeing BOMARC surface-to-air missile program that was a high priority within the Air Force at the time. *Lockheed Martin Skunk Works*

As plans for production progressed, the price of the Saturn crept upward. The original $85,000 estimate quickly climbed above $125,000 because of a combination of parts shortages, labor strife, and tooling problems. The Lockheed market survey had also missed one important item. At the end of World War II, the United States had the largest air force in the world, and little need for it. Thousands of relatively new aircraft were quickly retired by the armed services, including hundreds of Douglas C-47s (DC-3s) and C-54s (DC-4s), as well as Lockheed Lodestars and other small transports. Eventually, over 31,000 surplus aircraft were available on the civilian market. With the average C-47 carrying a price tag of less than $25,000, no airline was interested in an untried aircraft that cost five times as much, even if it might have been superior in terms of operating and maintenance costs. The timing was not right and the Model 75 was canceled. The two prototypes were broken up as scrap to allow Lockheed to write the project off of their corporate taxes.

The Model 89 Constitution

A second project that slightly predated the XP-80 effort was another transport—the Model 89 Constitution. As Johnson observed: "In this project we used the Skunk Works engineering methods, but we used conventional shop practices. . . . It ended up one of the world's most underpowered airplanes."

During World War II, Pan American World Airways was responsible for the long-range overseas transport of high-priority personnel and cargo. This was partially because Pan Am had an outstanding reputation as an overseas airline prior to the war. Pan Am also had the only aircraft and established bases that enabled such flights. Four separate projects were underway during the war to develop a truly long-range transport—the Douglas C-74, Boeing C-97, Convair C-99, and the Lockheed XR6O-1. The first three projects were under Army Air Forces jurisdiction, while the Lockheed project was managed by the Navy.

In response to the Navy requirement, Hibbard and Johnson outlined an aircraft capable of carrying a 20,000-pound payload over a range of 4,500 miles while cruising at 250 miles per hour at 25,000 feet. Lockheed engineer Jack Real collaborated with the legendary head of Pan

Am engineering, Andre Priester, to refine the requirements. They agreed upon a pressurized double-deck fuselage that could carry 204 military passengers; the civilian configuration would accommodate 51 day passengers and 58 sleeper berths along with 11 crew members. Pan Am initially expressed considerable interest in the design, although the situation would change as the war drew to a close. In the spring of 1943 the navy awarded Lockheed a $111,250,000 contract for 50 aircraft. A small team of 15 engineers was pulled from other Lockheed projects and assigned to rapidly develop an XR6O-1 prototype.

The XR6O-1 aircraft was to be powered by four new 5,500-shaft horsepower Wright "turbine propellers," known today as turboprops. Unfortunately, the military soon canceled the development of the Wright turboprop engines and forced Lockheed to use 3,000-horsepower Pratt & Whitney R4360-18 Wasp Major radial engines instead. This change delayed the first flight by over a year and resulted in an aircraft that was significantly underpowered. In reality, the aircraft had just half the power originally specified. Slightly more powerful versions of the Wasp Major were eventually fitted, but several proposals to retrofit other turboprop engines never came to fruition. As the war ended, the production contract was canceled, and only the two prototypes were left.

The two Constitutions were assigned to Navy Transport Squadron VR-44 at Naval Air Station (NAS) Alameda, California, in 1949. During 1950, one of the Constitutions had the distinction of being the first aircraft to show a full-length motion picture while in flight. The world premiere of *Slattery's Hurricane* was shown 10,000 feet over New York City. During 1951 Lockheed performed major overhauls on both aircraft, but the Navy suddenly decided that the Constitutions were too expensive to keep in service and declared them surplus in 1953. Two years later they were sold to private operators, but were denied airworthiness certificates. One languished in Las Vegas and the other at Opa-Locka, Florida, until they were scrapped in 1969 and 1979, respectively.

The first Navy program undertaken by Skunk Works was the XFV-1 vertical takeoff fighter. This was a truly unusual vehicle that used a 7,100-equivalent horsepower Allison YT40-A-14 turboshaft engine to drive a pair of counter-rotating propellers. The wingtip pods would have housed fuel and four 20-mm cannons in production versions, but were used for flight test instrumentation in the prototypes. *Tony Landis Collection*

The XF-90

The L-153 can trace its origins to mid-1945 during the XP-80 prototype effort when Johnson responded to an army request for an even more advanced fighter design. The initial response to the use of the Lockheed-developed L-1000 engines was less than enthusiastic, so a variety of Westinghouse and General Electric engines soon were evaluated.

Regardless of what engine was chosen, it was recognized that "tailpipe burning"—now called afterburning in the United States or reheat in Great Britain—would be required to provide any measure of performance. Johnson

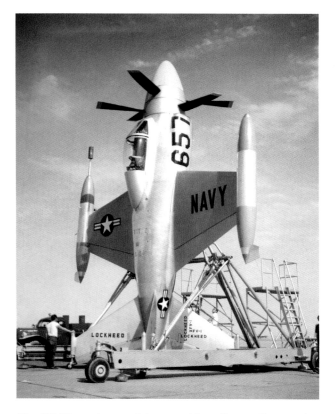

The XFV-1 used a special ground handling trailer to raise or lower it from its vertical launch position to a horizontal attitude for maintenance and storage. After the aircraft was raised, the trailer would disconnect from its attaching locations on the bottom of the wings and move out of the way. As it turned out, the aircraft never made a vertical takeoff or landing. Instead, a set of spiderlike auxiliary landing gear was attached to the lower fuselage and the aircraft was flown conventionally. A few vertical-to-horizontal (and vice versa) were made at a safe altitude, and clouds were usually used as make-believe landing fields. The primary rationale for this conservative flight test program was the general unreliability of the Allison engine. *Tony Landis Collection*

arranged to have an experimental afterburning engine installed in the second XP-80A and flown extensively by Tony LeVier. Things did not always go as planned, and LeVier had several harrowing moments while lighting the experimental afterburner. Both pilot and aircraft came through intact in all tests.

The XF-90 project was assigned to Palmer with Bill Ralston as his assistant, along with 36 engineers and shop mechanics. The Air Force authorized Lockheed to build two XP-90 prototypes on July 14, 1947, but by mid-1948 Johnson began to notice that the Skunk Works–type development effort that had worked so well on the XP-80 was running into considerable difficulty on the XF-90. Instead of building the prototypes in-house, they were being built by the mainstream manufacturing organization, resulting in significantly increased requirements for drawings and meetings. Eventually some compromises were reached, but the "hands-on" environment that had surrounded the XP-80, and would characterize future Skunk Works efforts, was missing from the XF-90. This project would represent one of the few failures in Skunk Works history.

Regardless of the difficulty, construction of the two aircraft continued, and on June 3, 1948, Tony LeVier made the XF-90's maiden flight using two non-afterburning Westinghouse XJ34 engines. A total of 17 flights were conducted over the next two months, but the aircraft was so underpowered that rocket-assisted take-off (RATO) bottles were required for almost every takeoff. The flights revealed a variety of handling and performance problems that took the rest of the year to resolve.

By the time the problems were taken care of, the Air Force had announced that the XF-90 was in competition with the McDonnell XF-88 and the North American XF-93 for any future production contract. The fly-off began in April 1950, and probably ranks as one of the most disorganized events in Air Force history. Besides the fact that none of the three competitors were ready to be compared against each other due to continuing development problems, the three aircraft had each been developed to very different specifications.

None of the aircraft, as originally built, would be produced, but the McDonnell XF-88 was declared the winner and would evolve into the F-101 Voodoo. The first XF-90 was sent to the NACA Lewis Laboratory in Cleveland, Ohio, for use as a structural test article, and its fate is unknown. The second aircraft still exists and is intact but highly radioactive after it was used as a test specimen for three different atomic tests in Nevada.

F-94 Starfire

Concurrently with the development of the XF-90, Hibbard and Johnson proposed various advanced versions of the venerable P-80 to the Air Force, and all were rejected. The appearance of a Tupolev Tu-4 Bull (a copy of the Boeing B-29) at the Soviet Aviation Day display at Tushino in 1947 changed everything. Continuing development problems with the Curtiss XP-87 Blackhawk and Northrop XP-89 Scorpion interceptors led the air force to ask Lockheed to expedite the development for a radar-equipped version of the two-seat T-33 trainer.

A formal contract with the Air Force to design the aircraft was signed on October 14, 1949, and Johnson assigned Rus Daniell to lead a team to handle preliminary design. The new Model 780 featured a revised nose that housed the components of the E-1 fire control system above and forward of four .50-caliber machine guns that were in the same general location as the lower four guns in the F-80. An afterburning version of the J33 engine was specified to compensate for the additional weight of the radar installation, and the vertical stabilizer was increased in height to regain the stability lost to the longer nose.

The straight-wing Model 780 seems like a step backwards from the swept-wing XF-90, but the new aircraft benefited greatly from the efforts expended by Palmer and his team on the XF-90. Much had been learned about the design and operation of afterburners during the XF-90 flight program and its supporting XP-80A testing; the use of 75ST (instead of 24ST) aluminum alloy had been pioneered on

the XF-90; and the viability of a unique control mixing system had been proven. All of these results would come in handy during the F-94 program.

Two TF-80Cs (T-33s) were supplied as prototypes, and in a typical Skunk Works effort, were rolled out less than 15 weeks later. Initially called ETF-80Cs, they were subsequently redesignated ET-33As, YF-94s, EYF-94s, and YF-94As; Lockheed named them Starfires. It should be noted that the aircraft, as presented at the rollout, had only been superficially modified. They lacked the E-1 fire control system, aft cockpit displays, and afterburning engine. LeVier took the first YF-94A on its maiden flight on April 16, 1949, with Glenn Fulkerson in the back seat. The urgency surrounding the program was extreme, and the Air Force quickly ordered 853 F-94As and slightly improved F-94Bs to be built by the mainstream Lockheed production facilities at Burbank and Palmdale, California.

Almost immediately after the Air Force ordered the F-94As, Johnson proposed an improved F-94 that incorporated an unguided rocket installation in place of the machine guns in the F-94A. In addition, the new L-188 included a revised wing and horizontal stabilizer, increased fuel capacity, an improved E-5 fire control system, and a more powerful Pratt & Whitney J48 engine. Except for the engine intakes and canopy, little remained of the original P-80 design. The Air Force was unimpressed, mainly because the F-89 promised to provide a much more capable platform if the bugs could ever be worked out. Not being ones to give up easily, Hibbard and Johnson convinced Lockheed management to privately fund a prototype of the new configuration. The investment had worked well for the T-33, so it was approved.

The initial flight testing of the new configuration was anything but trouble-free, but eventually LeVier and the engineers worked through the problems and developed an aircraft that LeVier later described as his favorite. Johnson's determination finally paid off, although the Air Force's decision was as much due to continued problems with the F-89 as to Lockheed's marketing. The Air Force

Both of the YC-130s (56-3396 and 56-3397) show that very little has changed in the 40-plus years since the type first flew. The most telling external change has been the addition of a larger radar unit on the nose. The YC-130s used three-bladed propellers instead of the production four-blade units. The two YC-130s were the only Herks to be built in Burbank. All production aircraft have been manufactured in Marietta, Georgia. *Tony Landis Collection*

subsequently purchased the L-188 demonstrator and designated it YF-97; this would later be changed to YF-94C.

Continued development problems delayed the F-94C's introduction into operational service by two years, but ultimately the mainstream Lockheed production facilities manufactured 234 F-94Cs. It was another case of the rapid-prototyping capabilities of a Skunk Works–type operation putting Lockheed in a position to capitalize on an urgent air force requirement.

The X-7

Surprisingly, given all of the advances in aerospace technology provided by Lockheed, until recently only had a single X-plane been even loosely associated with Skunk Works. At the end of 1946, Lockheed responded to an Army request for data concerning an unmanned high-speed aerodynamic and propulsion testbed. The government responded favorably to the Lockheed proposal and sent a letter of intent for Project MX-883 in January 1947. Willis Hawkins led a small team in designing the L-171 around a single Marquardt SRJ37-MN-1 ramjet, which was expected to be capable of maintaining speeds between Mach 2.3 and 3.0 for about 3 minutes. This was particularly significant given that Chuck Yeager had not yet flown the XS-1 above Mach 1; that would not occur until October 14, 1947.

During the design process, it became apparent that the small size of the L-171 (it was only 15 feet long) was forcing too many compromises in performance and payload. Hawkins and Irv Culver set aside the L-171 design and concentrated on a larger vehicle with better performance margins.

The X-7 program was too small to set up a dedicated group like the original XP-80 prototype effort, but the nature of the development also did not fit a normal Lockheed project organization. In the end, Lockheed left the development and manufacturing effort to a quasi-independent group attached to the Preliminary Design Department. Although Hawkins and Culver used much of the same philosophy that would become a Skunk Works trademark, the X-7 was not truly developed in a Skunk Works environment.

Hawkins and Culver succeeded in building a vehicle that proved very important in demonstrating various technologies, particularly the engines that were being developed for the Bomarc surface-to-air missile. Several one-third-scale X-7s were produced and tested, followed by the first full-scale X-7 flight on April 26, 1951. Approximately 130 test flights were recorded by the 30

X-7s manufactured, and several of the missiles logged more than 10 flights each, and were air-dropped from modified B-29 and B-50 carrier aircraft.

The X-7, particularly the later X-7A-3 variant equipped with Marquardt 36-inch-diameter ramjets, offered truly amazing performance. A maximum speed of Mach 4.31 (2,881 miles per hour) was attained on one flight, while another recorded a maximum altitude of 106,000 feet. Detailed knowledge of this flight regime would become important when the development of the famous Blackbirds began 10 years later.

During 1954, Lockheed founded the Missile Systems Division (later known as the Lockheed Missiles and Space Company—LMSC) at the old production test site in Van Nuys. Hibbard was named general manager of the new company, and Hawkins and the X-7 work were transferred to it. Most of the X-7 vehicles were actually built by LMSC. Eventually LMSC outgrew the Van Nuys facility and moved into new facilities in Sunnyvale, California, and would go on to develop a highly successful series of Navy submarine-launched ballistic missiles—the Polaris, Poseidon, and Trident. Although LMSC never produced an airplane, they developed a significant reputation in other areas.

The XFV-1

The 10 years immediately after World War II brought some innovative thinking to the aerospace industry, including Lockheed and Skunk Works. Many of the ideas were too advanced to be accomplished with available technology, but in many cases this did not stop industry and the military from trying. In 1947 Lockheed began to investigate a Navy requirement for a vertical takeoff and landing (VTOL) fighter to operate from the smaller aircraft carriers. The preliminary design team was headed by Art Flock with some assistance from Johnson. Again, the project was not performed in the same manner as the XP-80 prototypes had been, but some of the lessons learned from that effort were used.

The first XF-104 in later markings. Originally there was a simple Lockheed star on the forward fuselage instead of this white-and-red XF-104 marking. Herman "Fish" Salmon is shown climbing into the cockpit on the lakebed at Edwards AFB. The relatively narrow track of the main landing gear is apparent in this photo, but an abundance of available thrust meant the F-104 spent little time on the ground. *Tony Landis Collection*

Although externally similar in appearance, the two XF-104s were different from future production aircraft. The single 10,500-pounds-force Wright J65-B-6 ("B" stood for Buick who manufactured the engines initially used in the XF-104s) engine could not provide sufficient power to push the prototypes to reach Mach 2, and allowed them to use simple fixed inlets. The choice of the 17,000-pounds-force General Electric J79 for production aircraft would require many changes, but ultimately produced a much more capable fighter. This photo shows one of a series of engine run-up tests conducted during early 1954. *Tony Landis Collection*

By 1950 a competition was underway that pitted the Lockheed Model 81 against entries from Convair, Goodyear, Martin, and Northrop. The Convair Model 5 (XFY-1) was judged the most promising, but the Navy also provided funding to prototype the Lockheed Model 81 under the XFV-1 designation. The resulting aircraft was generally similar to its Convair competitor and used a single Allison XT40 turboprop engine to power counter-rotating three-bladed propellers. The aircraft was designed to sit vertically on a cruciform tail equipped with a castoring wheel on each tail surface tip. Although it was stubby, the aircraft presented a clean and modern appearance, typical of contemporary Lockheed designs.

The first XFV-1 was completed in early 1953 and Lockheed test pilot Herman "Fish" Salmon made its first official flight on June 16, 1954, and took off in a conventional manner using a long auxiliary landing gear attached to the fuselage. A total of 22 flights eventually accumulated 11.5 hours of flight time during a 10-month period, and the overall handling characteristics

of the unusual design were deemed to be satisfactory, but the 580-mile-per-hour top speed was disappointing. The engine proved unreliable and not powerful enough to ever attempt vertical landings or takeoffs, although many successful transitions were made in and out of vertical hovers while at a safe altitude.

The Convair design had largely the same lack of success, and with a top speed of under 600 miles per hour, neither design was deemed adequate as a fighter. Continuing development problems with the Allison engine eventually resulted in the navy canceling the effort in mid-1955. The second XFV-1 had not even been completed, and the airframe later served as a gate guard at NAS Los Alamitos before being transferred to the Naval Aviation Museum at NAS Pensacola. The first airframe was given to Hiller Aircraft to use for parts in their X-18 til-trotor program.

Turboprop Connies

The Constellation remains one of the most aesthetically pleasing airliners ever developed, even though it was less than a complete commercial success. Similar to the Model 75 Saturn, the Connie's major failing was that it had to compete against a great many surplus military transports in the immediate postwar era.

The problem was compounded when the deHavilland Comet took to the air in 1949. This was the first all-jet transport, and although it would suffer an agonizing development and service career, it clearly pointed out that piston-powered transports were rapidly becoming obsolete. However, it was not yet obvious that pure-jet aircraft were the wave of the future. Faced with the choice of committing to an expensive program to develop an all-jet transport, or to take a more conservative intermediate approach and re-engine the Constellation with turboprop engines, Lockheed chose the latter—it was not a good choice.

The military was also interested in a turboprop version of the Super Constellation, which was in production as the R7V for the Navy and C-121 for the Air Force. Palmer and Johnson were assigned to adapt the Pratt & Whitney T34 turboprop to the Super Constellation airframe. Fortunately, Lockheed had thought ahead and all Super Constellations had been built to handle more powerful engines, so the major task was optimizing the shape of the new nacelle and integrating the new engines with existing electrical and hydraulic systems.

Two R7V-1s were pulled from the production line, equipped with prototype YT34 turboprops driving wide-chord three-bladed propellers, and redesignated R7V-2. The first R7V-2 made its maiden flight on September 1, 1954. Shortly, two additional R7V-1s were equipped with production T34 engines and transferred to the Air Force as YC-134s (soon redesignated YC-121Fs). These aircraft were capable of cruising at 440 miles per hour, which made them the fastest propeller-driven aircraft in the world at the time. The two R7V-2s were used for a variety of tests, both military and of a commercial derivative. The two YC-121Fs joined four other Air Force aircraft equipped with T34 engines (two Boeing YC-97Js and two Douglas YC-124Bs) for in-service evaluations. Military interest in the T34 waned during 1954, and the only production aircraft ever equipped with the engine was the short-lived Douglas C-133 Cargomaster.

Lockheed extensively marketed the T-34-powered Model 1249 Super Constellation, but found no takers among the airlines. Eventually, the four turboprop Connies were retired and used for parts to keep several piston-powered Constellations flying. The future of commercial aviation lay in the pure-jet designs such as the Boeing 707 and Douglas DC-8, and Lockheed was left out of the first round of jetliners.

The RB-69

One of the least-known Air Force aircraft of the late 1950s was also one of the least-known Skunk Works efforts. The effort was particularly significant since it was probably Lockheed's first contract from the Central Intelligence Agency (CIA), and predated the U-2 effort by a few months. Johnson assigned Luther McDonald to extensively modify seven P2V-7 Neptune antisubmarine patrol aircraft into covert intelligence-gathering aircraft. The effort was called Project WILD CHERRY by the CIA, and was handled in a classic Skunk Works fashion, although the official Skunk Works had not been formed yet.

The aircraft were equipped with a variety of unique systems, including the first operational terrain avoidance radar (built by Texas Instruments) and a Singer Doppler navigation radar. A variety of electronic countermeasures (ECM) equipment was also carried, and several were modified years later with a General Electric side-looking airborne radar (SLAR) in a large housing on the right side of the fuselage.

Initial missions, in 1955 and 1956, were flown from Wiesbaden, Germany, mainly to map the Russian power grid in Eastern Europe. Beginning in 1957 missions were flown over China from bases in Taiwan, usually with Taiwanese crews and markings. The intelligence gathered on these missions was later used to plan U-2 missions over the same territory. The missions over China expanded to include dropping leaflets, and later, to inserting agents from a special compartment in the bomb bay. At least four of the RB-69s were shot down over China before the type was removed from service in 1964.

The C-130

In 1951, Hawkins and Art Flock were handed an assignment that would result in the aircraft that has enjoyed Lockheed's longest continuous production run. They would use the same basic rules that had been applied to the XP-80 prototype effort—ones that became Skunk Works trademarks. It began on February 2, 1951, when the Air Force issued a request for proposals for a turboprop transport. Hawkins and Flock had only 60 days to develop a preliminary design for the L-206.

The proposal that was submitted in April 1951 detailed a four-engined aircraft that bore a slight resemblance to the

Often dubbed "a missile with a man in it" because of its short wingspan, the F-104 was a capable performer at all altitudes. The prototypes carried a variety of different tip-tanks in an effort to find a design that produced minimal drag and separated cleanly when jettisoned. Note the lack of the vertical fin on the tanks that would mark production units. *Tony Landis Collection*

Model 75 Saturn. Like the Saturn, the new aircraft used a high wing and a low fuselage. This design feature allowed easy access for personnel and equipment. A rear loading ramp allowed vehicles to directly drive on and off the aircraft; alternately, the ramp could be lowered to a horizontal position to allow trucks to offload onto a flat surface.

It is interesting to note that Johnson was not happy with the proposed aircraft, and he refused to sign off on the proposal. Hibbard, Johnson's boss, eventually overruled him and the proposal was submitted on schedule. It was a good thing because the Lockheed proposal was selected over ones from Boeing, Douglas, and Fairchild. It took three years before the first flight, accomplished with the second of the two prototypes, on August 23, 1954, with Stanley Beltz, Roy Wimmer, Jack Real, and Dick Stanton in the cockpit. The first aircraft was being used as a static test article, but would ultimately fly on January 21, 1955. Testing quickly confirmed that the

C-130 was a good aircraft, and the air force ordered seven production models.

During the early 1950s, Lockheed had requested permission to reopen the facility at Marietta, Georgia, where Bell had assembled B-29 Superfortresses. Initially this facility was used by Lockheed to refurbish a large fleet of stored B-29s for use in the Korean War, and to construct 394 Boeing-designed B-47 Stratojets. With this project coming to an end and the Burbank facility running out of room, Lockheed decided to move C-130 production to Marietta. The result is that only the two YC-130s were manufactured in Burbank, and Marietta has been producing the Hercules constantly for the last 45 years.

The Starfighter

Perhaps more than any other aircraft during the pre–Skunk Works years, the F-104 Starfighter best represents Johnson and the engineers at Lockheed. The F-104 would never be truly embraced by the U.S. Air Force, but 2,579 of the aircraft would serve over a dozen other countries for up to 40 years.

In November 1952, Lockheed sent an unsolicited proposal for the lightweight Mach 2 fighter to the Air Force where it generated sufficient interest to result in a design competition. Proposals were received from Lockheed, North American, Northrop, and Republic, but it was mostly a foregone conclusion that the Lockheed design would be chosen. On March 12, 1952, a letter contract was issued for two XF-104 prototypes under Weapons System WS-303A.

The CL-246 was a product of the Preliminary Design Department under the direction of Hibbard and Johnson. In order to expedite the design and construction of the two prototypes, the technique that had proven so successful with the XP-80 effort was replicated. With Palmer and Bill Ralston in charge, the full-scale mockup was ready for inspection on April 30, and the first prototype was rolled out of the shop 355 days after the project had been started. Not as quick as the XP-80, but the XF-104 was a more sophisticated aircraft.

During the late 1960s and early 1970s, Skunk Works promoted a significantly revised version of the Starfighter known as the CL-1200 Lancer. Shown here in its early stages, the Lancer used most of the F-104 fuselage mated with a new wing and empennage. Later it would evolve into the X-27 with new intakes and a larger, more sophisticated wing. This aircraft was designed with the same philosophy that resulted in various advanced Northrop F-5 designs—lightweight fighters do not need to be marginal performers. An advanced J79 engine was expected to allow the Lancer to keep up with most contemporary fighters. *Tony Landis Collection*

One of the major design features of the XF-104 was its wings, or lack thereof, that gave rise to the phrase "missile with a man in it." The wing extended only 7 feet on each side of the fuselage and was remarkably thin; the leading edge was so sharp that plastic covers were used to protect maintenance personnel while the XF-104 was on the ground. The wing also represented one of the largest unknowns during the early development effort since it was thinner than any wing that had flown at that time on a high-performance aircraft, including the X-7 research rocket. The XF-104 program spent almost 15 percent of its entire budget studying high-speed flutter and aeroelastic problems, thus contributing to the overall knowledge of the subject within the aerospace community.

The first of the two XF-104s made its official maiden flight on March 4, 1954, with LeVier at the controls. A landing gear malfunction kept the flight short, but LeVier landed without serious incident. Flight testing proceeded rapidly, and the second aircraft achieved Mach 1.79 (1,324 miles per hour) on March 25, 1955, and was flown by Ray Goudey. Overall, the three-year test program was deemed successful and the Air Force ordered 17 service test YF-104As, 147 production F-104As, and 26 two-seat F-104Bs. As with the P-80, the production models would be manufactured by the mainstream Lockheed production organization, and Skunk Works' involvement with the program ended, but Johnson's rise continued. In 1952 he was named chief engineer for Lockheed, a promotion from his previous position as chief research engineer. In his new position, Johnson would manage the activities of 5,500 people, including about 1,000 engineers. He would also be the inspiration behind two of Skunk Works' most important projects.

Two

The addition of the superpods on each wing greatly increased the volume available to carry sensors. The superpods significantly alter the appearance of the U-2R, but fortunately have little impact on the aircraft's handling. Although the initial years of service were flown without the superpods, today almost all missions require superpods of some description, and there are a variety of configurations available depending upon the desired sensor load. *Lockheed Martin Skunk Works photo by Eric Schulzinger*

The Spy Planes—
DRAGON LADIES AND BLACKBIRDS

Dragon Ladies

The U-2 established the Skunk Works. Although Johnson was already well-known, it was the CIA's decision to let Lockheed design and build the U-2 that cemented Skunk Works' reputation.

During December 1953, for reasons that are not completely clear, Johnson had begun exploring the feasibility of modifying the basic XF-104 design into a high-altitude reconnaissance platform. By March 1954 this had resulted in the CL-282. Belatedly, Johnson submitted the design to the Air Force as part of Project MX-2147, code-named BALD EAGLE. The Air Force conducted a somewhat hurried review and decided the competing Bell Model 67 better suited its requirements; on June 7, 1954, Johnson was informed that his proposal had been rejected.

In the meantime, the CIA had discovered that the military services could not be depended upon to provide detailed reconnaissance whenever and wherever the CIA wanted it; conflicting priorities within the military and interagency rivalry were the primary reasons. Since the Soviet Union was embarking on an ambitious program to develop long-range missiles equipped with nuclear warheads, the CIA considered on-demand intelligence critical. The obvious answer was to create a private air arm—an opportunity not lost on Johnson.

On November 19, 1954, Johnson discussed a modified CL-282 with the intelligence community. The proposal generated a great deal of interest, granted that Lockheed could deliver the aircraft quickly. Following in the tradition that began with the XP-80 prototype effort, Johnson promised the first aircraft would fly by September 1955—less than a year in the future. Two days later Johnson met with senior Lockheed management and convinced them to allow him to design and manufacture the aircraft. This was a departure from the past when production was turned over to the mainstream Lockheed organization. In this case Johnson deemed it necessary to keep the project totally in-house to preserve its secrecy and meet the promised schedule. His bosses agreed and a dynasty was born.

At the end of November the CIA formally approved the project under the code name AQUATONE, and a $54 million contract for 20 aircraft was signed on December 9, 1954, although Johnson would later return almost $8 million of this due to cost underruns. By the end of 1954,

A late photo of the Burbank plant. At various times Skunk Works had occupied Plant B-5, shown as a group of Quonset-type buildings in the upper right corner; and Plant B-6, the large complex just to the left of the control tower in the center. *Lockheed Martin Skunk Works*

Johnson and his team of 25 engineers and 81 shop personnel began working 100-hour weeks in order to meet the schedule. While Johnson did eventually obtain additional personnel, he never had more than 80 engineers working on the U-2 project. The design was technologically demanding since minimum weight and drag were essential. On December 10, one day after the contract was signed, the AQUATONE design was frozen, and 10 days later construction of production tooling had begun. Around this time the aircraft became known within Skunk Works as "Kelly's Angel" or simply as "Angel." The individual aircraft would be known as "articles."

Midmorning on July 24, 1955, the first U-2A arrived at the test location at Groom Lake, better known to Lockheed personnel at the time as the "Test Location," or "The Ranch." Groom Lake has been the subject of much speculation and many rumors over the years, and is located inside a restricted area (Area 51) near the nuclear

test site run by the Department of Energy (originally, the Atomic Energy Commission). It is located approximately 100 miles northwest of Las Vegas, Nevada.

The first flight of the U-2 came on August 4, 1955, with LeVier at the controls. Four days later, on August 8, LeVier made the "official" first flight in front of senior CIA officials, and on October 18, 1955, the U-2 achieved its design altitude of 73,000 feet. When the program's one-year anniversary arrived on December 1, 1955, Skunk Works had already delivered four aircraft and had five more in the assembly jigs.

In December 1955 Skunk Works received the go-ahead for a further 30 aircraft, bringing the total to 50. Again, Johnson managed to underrun the contract, and returned almost $2 million to the government. After production was completed, five more aircraft were built, mostly from spare parts with only some minor systems (and engines) being funded anew. An interesting fact is that most of the U-2s were not built at the Lockheed plant in Burbank. The main plant was busy building P2V Neptune antisubmarine aircraft for the Navy and T-33 trainers for the Air Force, so U-2 production was set up in a building 90 miles north of Burbank in Oildale, just outside Bakersfield, that had originally built subassemblies for the C-121 transport. The facility began constructing U-2s in January 1956, and by the end of the year there were 400 people, mainly local laborers, working there. The U-2s were completely assembled and checked out inside the building at Oildale, and then were partially disassembled and trucked to the local airport for transport to Groom Lake inside C-124s. By the end of 1957, the plant was closed and U-2 production was complete for the time being.

By the end of its fourth year in operation, the CIA considered the U-2 to be the single most important technical intelligence gathering means in the inventory. U-2 flights had revealed the fallacy of the Soviet jet bomber threat, the true number of Soviet ICBMs, and had underscored the shortcomings of Soviet technology

The first U-2 at Groom Lake prior to its first flight. The aircraft arrived at the test location on July 24, 1955, and made its first flight on August 4, so this photo was taken sometime between those dates. Note the extremely small size of the rear wheels and the location of the jettisonable outriggers at midspan. The rear tires were solid rubber and not pneumatic like most aircraft tires. The only exterior markings were national insignias and the small "001" on the vertical stabilizer. *Lockheed Martin Skunk Works*

in general. However, it was an understanding based on a very limited sample.

In the 48-month period ending in December 1960, only 40 excursions over Soviet territory had been completed by Operation OVERFLIGHT. In addition to excellent photography, these missions also deployed the PURPLEFLASH seismic sensor system around the Soviet Lop Nor nuclear test site. Most of the U-2 missions, however, were conducted around the periphery of denied territory using oblique angles at ranges approaching 100 miles. Intelligence flights were not confined to the Soviet Union. Egypt, Iraq, Lebanon, Saudi Arabia, Syria, and Yemen were all targets for the U-2, and on December 6, 1958, overflights began over the Chekiang and Kaingsi provinces of China—a location that would be visited frequently in the future. Even so, it was obvious that the U-2's days as an overflight vehicle were numbered.

The Type-A camera installation consisted of three Fairchild HR-732 cameras with 24-inch focal length lenses. Generally one camera was angled to each side of the aircraft while the middle camera pointed straight down, but the package could be configured to have all three pointing at nadir. The Type-A configuration carried 1,800 feet of film for each camera and provided a ground resolution of 2 to 8 feet. The interchangeable payloads in the Q bay were a major feature of the U-2 design. *Lockheed Martin Skunk Works*

Article 349 (65-6682) was transferred to NASA in June 1971 and assigned to the High Altitude Air Aircraft Program at the NASA Ames Research Center. The blue, gray, and white paint scheme used by NASA was a striking contrast from the all-black CIA and Air Force aircraft. NASA used two U-2Cs until April 1989 when both were retired and replaced by ER-2 versions of the U-2R. *Lockheed Martin Skunk Works photo by Eric Schulzinger*

Before U-2 flights over the Soviet Union ended, however, there would be one flight that caused considerable embarrassment for the CIA and United States. On May 1, 1960, Francis Gary Powers, a veteran of 27 CIA U-2 missions, was assigned to photograph two major ICBM test locations at Sverdlovsk and Plesetck. Not coincidentally, these were also the locations of some of the heaviest air defenses in the world.

Powers' mission was routine until he began his photo run 67,000 feet over Sverdlovsk. Powers reported feeling a dull explosion underneath and behind the aircraft and watching the sky turn a bright orange. Later analysis by Johnson indicated the horizontal stabilizers had probably been badly damaged. Moments later, the main wing structure failed and both wings separated from the fuselage. The physical damage to the aircraft pinned Powers' legs under the instrument panel and eliminated any possibility of ejecting, but he managed to bail out without using the seat. Powers was captured and put on trial in the Soviet Union. This was the U-2's most visible

This shot illustrates the substantial difference in size between the original U-2 (left) and the U-2R. There is no mistaking that both aircraft are U-2s. The U-2R was a result of the need for additional aircraft since 40 of the original 55 U-2s have been lost to various causes, including the 5 shot down over China, 1 over Cuba, and several over and around the Soviet Union. Also, heavier sensors and additional ECM equipment had taken a large performance toll on the origianl aircraft. The late U-2C had less than half the range of the original U-2A and its maximum altitude had decreased by over 5,000 feet. *Lockheed Martin Skunk Works*

moment. Powers would be released by the Soviets two years later, but the damage was done. U-2 overflights of Soviet territory ceased. Since the U-2s were providing approximately 90 percent of the hard photographic data on the Soviet Union, this severely hampered U.S. intelligence operations until the CORONA reconnaissance satellites were perfected. Powers himself was hired by Johnson as a test pilot and held that position until he retired in 1976. A year later Powers was killed while flying a television traffic helicopter in Los Angeles.

Although the U-2C was still providing valuable intelligence, the continued incorporation of more and heavier sensors and ECM equipment was rapidly taking its toll on performance. Late in its life, the U-2C had less than half the range of the original U-2As, and its maximum altitude had decreased by almost 5,000 feet. Additionally, over 40 of the original 55 airframes had been lost to various causes, including at least 5 that were shot down over China, one over Cuba, and several over and around the Soviet Union. Despite the pending development of the Blackbird, something would have to be done about the U-2s.

U-2 Versions

There were nine versions of the basic U-2 that were allocated official designations beginning with the initial 53 production U-2A-1-LOs. With the exception of the two purpose-built U-2D aircraft, all subsequent small-wing U-2s were converted from one of these aircraft.

Five modified WU-2A-1-LOs (Articles 381–385) had dedicated gas and particulate sampling systems installed in the Q bay and a "hard nose" containing a small intake valve assembly for the sampling mission. Some sources list these aircraft as U-2A-2-LOs.

The U-2B was a proposed bomber version of the Dragon Lady. These aircraft were to be equipped with a tricycle landing gear with the nose gear located in the normal main gear location in the fuselage and the new forward retracting main gear located in large wing pods. Two hard-points would be located under each wing, and a single M60 gun would be carried on a trapeze located in the Q bay for self-defense. Other variations of this concept would be considered over the years, including ones using the larger U-2R airframe, but none ever made it past paper studies and wind tunnel testing. There were numerous other proposals for U-2 variants that were not proceeded with, such as in December 1964 when Johnson proposed a tanker based on the U-2 airframe that could refuel other U-2s at 70,000 feet.

Over the years, all surviving U-2As were converted to the U-2C-1-LO standard. This included a more powerful J75 engine and larger air intakes. The first converted aircraft (Article 342) made its maiden flight in the new configuration on May 13, 1959. There were two purpose-built U-2D-1-LO aircraft (388 and 394) that were unique in being the only production two-seat versions of the original U-2. In 1961, three U-2As (Articles 347, 354, and 355) were equipped with flying-boom aerial refueling systems and redesignated U-2E-1-LO. Two U-2Cs (Articles 370 and 374) were equipped with aerial refueling systems and redesignated U-2F-1-LO. The three U-2Es were also redesignated U-2F-1-LO when they were re-engined with J75s, making a total of five U-2Fs.

In one of the more interesting conversions, three U-2Cs (348, 349, and 362) were equipped with arresting hooks and other specialized equipment and redesignated U-2G-1-LO. Lockheed was asked in May 1963 to study using a U-2 for naval operations, and in July a CIA U-2A was modified by adding three longerons to the aft fuselage, a faired tail hook ahead of the tail wheel, and cable guards in front of the main wheels. The main landing gear strut was also modified to allow it to swivel sideways to ease maneuvering around the carrier's elevators and hanger deck.

A further modification of the U-2G, the single U-2H-1-LO, was a carrier-equipped U-2C capable of aerial refueling. All of this extra equipment had an adverse effect on the aircraft's performance, and it spent most of its time at North Edwards being used for training and equipment testing.

An alarming rate of pilot attrition during flight training demonstrated the need for a two-seat version of the U-2. Two airframes (Articles 359 and 393) were modified with a raised second cockpit on top of the Q bay and used for pilot familiarization. These U-2C(T)-1-LOs were not considered operationally capable. Interestingly, these were the longest surviving original U-2s to serve the air force until U-2R trainers were available from the last production run in the 1980s.

The U-2R was essentially a new aircraft, and almost 40 percent larger than the original U-2 with a 23-foot increase in wingspan. Missions in excess of 14 hours became possible; the U-2R's ferry range of just over 8,000 miles is almost 3,000 miles greater than the U-2C's and essentially the same as the original U-2A's. The aircraft were equipped with the same 17,000-pounds-thrust Pratt & Whitney J75-P-13B engines used in the later U-2Cs. The first U-2R made its maiden flight on August 28, 1967, and all of the original dozen aircraft were delivered by December 1968.

The next aircraft to be developed, the TR-1A, was essentially identical to the U-2R, and was subsequently redesignated U-2R. Only minor changes had been made to the TR-1A when the production line re-opened. The same J75-P-13B engine was used, but these engines came from retired F-105 and F-106 fighters and were modified by Pratt & Whitney for the high-altitude role. The most telling change was the horizontal stabilizer. The stabilizer needed to be strengthened on the original dozen U-2Rs and resulted in a series of small external ribs being added. These ribs were incorporated internally on the TR-1s. This, however, is an unreliable source of identification since the rear fuselages are frequently swapped between aircraft by maintenance crews. The first TR-1 was rolled out in Palmdale on July 15, 1981, and made its

The U-2F general arrangement diagram from the 1968 edition of the U-2C/F flight manual. The U-2F was essentially a U-2C fitted for aerial refueling, although a few systems were rearranged in order to accommodate the refueling equipment. The external fuel tanks could not be refilled in flight. *U.S. Air Force*

This is one of the more unusual paint schemes applied to the U-2 during its career. According to Jay Miller in his book *Skunk Works: The Official History*, this polka-dot pattern was apparently used to test reconnaissance satellite sensors. The aircraft is a CIA U-2C, N805X. *Lockheed Martin Skunk Works*

maiden flight on August 1. All TR-1As were subsequently redesignated U-2R in October 1991.

A two-seat version of the TR-1, designated TR-1B was also produced and used as a transition trainer much like the earlier U-2C(T)s had been. Unlike the earlier two-seaters, these aircraft were built from the beginning with two seats and weren't modified from single-seat aircraft. Two TR-1Bs and a single identical U-2R(T) were produced, and all were subsequently redesignated U-2R(T).

The U-2S designation came from installing the 18,300-pounds-thrust General Electric F118-GE-101 turbofan into the remaining U-2Rs. This engine saved 1,300 pounds and provided 16 percent better fuel economy than the J75, allowing a 1,400-mile increase in range. At the same time, wiring and mounting provisions for the various sensor systems were standardized so that all aircraft would be capable of carrying the entire variety of sensors. Previously, some aircraft were modified for specific sensors while others were not greatly complicating tasking. The first modified U-2S made its first flight on August 12, 1994, and all aircraft were modified by the end of 1998.

(The ER-1 designation was unofficially applied, somewhat after the fact, to a pair of U-2Cs that had been operated by NASA.)

An interesting fact to note is that the first of the final production batch of U-2s was actually delivered to NASA as an ER-2. Subsequently one other aircraft was delivered, and for a time NASA also operated a TR-1A on loan from the Air Force. These aircraft have also been modified to U-2S standards, although they retain their ER-2 designation. The first ER-2 was delivered on June 10, 1981, and the second followed in 1989.

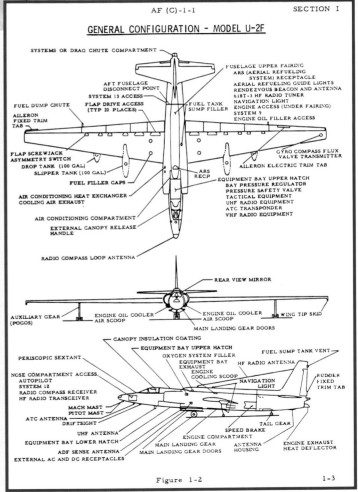

AF (C)-1-1   SECTION I

GENERAL CONFIGURATION - MODEL U-2F

Figure 1-2   1-3

Below:
When the U-2R (called TR-1s at the time) production line was reopened in 1979, the Air Force also ordered two dual-control TR-1B aircraft, as well as a single U-2R(T) using "black funds." The two-seat U-2s are not considered operationally capable since they do not have a Q bay to carry sensors and are not fitted with superpods on the wings. Nevertheless, they play an extremely important role in keeping the U-2 force operationally ready by providing pilot conversion and currency training. *Lockheed Martin Skunk Works photo by Eric Schulzinger*

Above:
The U.S. Navy borrowed two U-2Rs from the CIA to investigate their use as an experimental electronics platform (EP-X). One of the U-2Rs (Article 060) was finished in mostly natural metal with a light gray paint on the bottom of the fuselage to protect it against seawater splashing. The other aircraft (Article 061) was painted in the standard BLACK VELVET scheme used by the CIA and air force. Other U-2Rs were operated (not during the EP-X program) from aircraft carriers, particularly the USS *America* (CVA-66). Lockheed pilot Bill Park demonstrated that the U-2R could take off in less than 300 feet with only 20 knots of wind across the deck, and could reliably snag arresting wires during landing. All U-2Rs included provisions to fold the outer 6 feet of each wing, usually to fit in standard Air Force hangers, but this also helped aboard carriers. *Lockheed Martin Skunk Works*

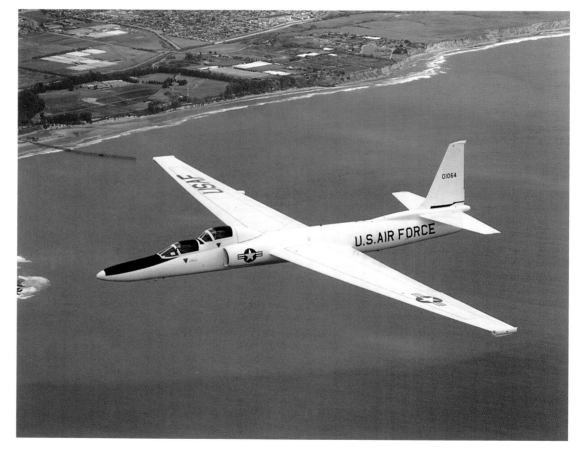

THE SPY PLANES

Big-Wing U-2s

In August 1966 Skunk Works was awarded a contract for the development of the CL-351. The model was referred to as U-2R, with the "R" meaning "redesigned" or "revised"; the designation became official somewhat later. The U-2R was almost 40 percent larger than the original U-2, with a 23-foot increase in wingspan. Missions in excess of 14 hours became possible, and the U-2R has a ferry range of just over 8,000 miles—almost 3,000 miles greater than the U-2C and essentially the same as the original U-2A.

Although Lockheed had anticipated a large production contract for the new U-2, budget and political considerations resulted in only 12 aircraft being ordered in September 1966. Of these, 6 were for the CIA and 6 for the Air Force. Unlike the original U-2 production, the U-2R would be manufactured at the Lockheed plant in Burbank. Lockheed test pilot Bill Park made the first flight on August 28, 1967, from the CIA facility at North Base on the edge of Edwards AFB. The second U-2R arrived at North Base in February 1968 and training of both CIA and air force pilots commenced. By December 1968, all 12 aircraft had been delivered. The production tooling was removed from Burbank during 1969 and placed in storage at Norton AFB in California.

Johnson wanted to produce more than a dozen U-2Rs. In a near desperate attempt during 1974 to keep the U-2R production line open, he proposed a "U-2R RPV" to compete with the forthcoming COMPASS COPE remotely piloted vehicles. The Air Force had decided that unmanned vehicles were the wave of the future and was ready to commit large amounts of funding to procure advanced high-performance RPVs. Primarily because it was based on an aircraft that already was in production, Lockheed argued that the U-2R RPV could be built for substantially less money than either of its competitors, and that it could accomplish the proposed mission more effectively. Although four COMPASS COPE

A flock of Blackbirds at Beale AFB just prior to retirement. The lone SR-71C trainer is in the extreme back and readily distinguishable by its short rear fuselage. This aircraft had been assembled late in the program by taking the surviving portions of the first YF-12A (which had been written off in an accident) and mating them with the forward fuselage from the nonflying structural test article. Rumors have it that the fuselage was not quite square and the aircraft was universally disliked by the pilots, therefore it was used only when the sole surviving SR-71B trainer was down for maintenance. The other 10 aircraft in the photo are SR-71As. *Lockheed Martin Skunk Works photo by Eric Schulzinger*

prototypes were built (two Boeing YQM-94As and two Teledyne Ryan YQM-98As), a combination of technical, economic, and political problems ended the program prematurely. This also spelled the end of the U-2R RPV, and no production contract was forthcoming.

The changing environment in Europe would come to Lockheed's rescue. A perceived need for increased tactical reconnaissance capability in Europe during the mid-1970s led the Pentagon to assign a group of air force and army officers to evaluate the reconnaissance

Above: An unpainted U-2R shows how the fuselage looks in primer and without the nose and wings. Special wheeled trailers like the one the fuselage is sitting on are used extensively when the aircraft is undergoing heavy maintenance. The construction of the U-2R is very conventional with few exotic alloys or composites being used. *Lockheed Martin Skunk Works*

Right: A pair of U-2Rs showing the ASARS-2 (advanced synthetic aperture radar system) nose. Similar to the Q bay and superpods, the nose of the U-2R can be changed to accommodate special sensors as needed. The ASARS-2 nose has a distinctive scoop on top that ducts air to the heat exchanger that is used to control the temperature of the system inside. A large antenna occupies most of the fairing, while mission electronics sit in the back third of the nose. These aircraft are seen after having returned from the Gulf War. *Lockheed Martin Skunk Works photo by Denny Lombard*

needs for the immediate future. The group concluded that the U-2 was the best platform, and the FY79 defense budget was changed to provide funds to restart the U-2 production line.

The initial $10.2 million contract called for the refurbishment of the old U-2R production tooling that had been placed in storage during 1969, along with new and replacement tooling manufactured as required. On November 16, 1979, after an almost 12-year lapse, the production of new U-2Rs (designated TR-1 at the time) began at the Palmdale location. A $42.4 million production contract for two Air Force TR-1As and a single NASA ER-2 was signed in October 1979. These aircraft were slightly updated versions of the original U-2R design. This was followed by orders for 35 more aircraft at a total cost of approximately $550 million.

Following a public rollout at Lockheed's Palmdale facility on July 15, 1981, the first TR-1A made its maiden flight on August 1, 1981, with Lockheed test pilot Ken Weir at the controls. By the time production ended, Lockheed had delivered 37 new aircraft. The three trainers were the first aircraft to be delivered—two TR-1Bs and a single identical U-2R(T) using black (secret) funding. Thirty-four single-seaters were built—2 ER-2s for NASA, 7 U-2Rs using black funding, and twenty-25 TR-1As. All of the TR-1As were redesignated U-2R in October 1991.

The first truly major improvement to the U-2R came when the Pratt & Whitney J75 engine was replaced with a version of the General Electric F118-GE-101 turbofan (called the F101-GE-F29 at the time) that was being developed for the then still-classified Northrop B-2 stealth bomber. The first modified U-2S made its maiden flight with Lockheed test pilot Weir at the controls on May 23, 1989. Oddly, this was four months before the B-2 first took flight. Besides the new engine, all U-2S aircraft were equipped with an improved electrical system, digital autopilot, and an auxiliary spoiler

activation system. All remaining U-2s, including four of the original 12 U-2Rs built 1967–68, were re-engined by the end of 1998.

In 1998, U-2S and ER-2 aircraft claimed four altitude and payload records. Three of the records were previously held by aircraft from the Soviet Union, and the fourth was a new world record. The aircraft used were not specially modified variants, but were standard mission-configured aircraft conducting routine flights. In early 2000, the total U-2S/ER-2 inventory consisted of

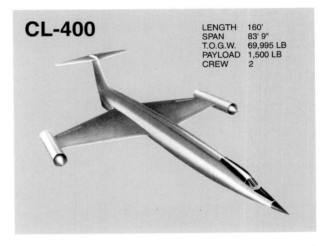

CL-400

LENGTH	160'
SPAN	83' 9"
T.O.G.W.	69,995 LB
PAYLOAD	1,500 LB
CREW	2

Project SUNTAN was an attempt to develop an operational aircraft powered by liquid hydrogen. The proposed air vehicle was the CL-400; an early example is shown here. This project actually progressed far enough that a full-scale mockup was built, along with various test specimens such as a liquid hydrogen tank and subscale wing panels. In the end the program proved too advanced for the available funding and was canceled. In many regards the money spent on SUNTAN was not wasted. Much of the engineering data was turned over to Convair and was used to create the Centaur upper stage that is still in use on Atlas and Titan launch vehicles. *Lockheed Martin Skunk Works*

37 aircraft. During 1998, the latest year for which statistics are available, the aircraft flew more than 13,640 hours without any accidents. Missions are routinely flown in support of a variety of agencies, including NASA, the U.S. military, Federal Emergency Management Agency, National Oceanic and Atmospheric Administration, Drug Enforcement Agency, NATO, and various universities.

Kelly's Blackbirds

Part of the reason Skunk Works had such a hard time interesting the CIA and Air Force in more U-2s is that something much different was on the drawing boards. On April 26, 1962, Lockheed test pilot Lou Schalk made the first flight in an aircraft that was far more advanced than anything in the sky, and when it was made public several years later, this aircraft would capture the world's fascination like few other aircraft ever have. Three distinct variants were eventually manufactured, but surprisingly, none of them ever had an

ARCHANGEL II was the second in the "A" series of design studies conducted under the OXCART project that eventually produced the A-12 Blackbird. This configuration was powered by two turbojet engines under the wings at midspan and two ramjets on the wingtips. Unlike the competing Convair FISH configuration, this design had no radar-defeating features. *Lockheed Martin Skunk Works*

An A-12 sits parked in front of the OXCART hangers at Groom Lake. The distinctive natural metal and black paint scheme was initially applied to all of the OXCART aircraft and the YF-12As. The black covers the high-temperature plastic composite areas of the wing leading edges and fuselage chines, as well as the composite vertical stabilizers. The black paint was extended around the canopy partially to provide better heat radiance and as an antiglare shield. *Lockheed Martin Skunk Works*

official name. Unofficially, they have all been referred to as "Blackbirds" and "Habu," the fastest, highest flying air-breathing aircraft in the world. The Lockheed model number of the original CIA variant was A-12, but by a sort of inspired perversity it came to be called OXCART, a code name also applied to the program under which it was developed. The other two variants carried the Air Force designations YF-12 and SR-71.

In late 1957 the CIA asked Skunk Works to determine how the probability of shooting down an aircraft varied with respect to its speed, altitude, and radar cross-section (RCS). This analysis demonstrated that supersonic speed greatly reduced the chances of detection by radar. The probability of being shot down was not reduced to zero, but it was evident that high-speed overflight was worth serious consideration. Working with Johnson, the CIA drew up the basic requirements for a U-2 successor, an aircraft with a Mach 3+ cruising speed at altitudes in excess of 80,000 feet. By September 1958, Lockheed had studied a number of possible configura-

tions. Some were based on ramjet engines, and others on both ramjets and turbojets. Engineers at Skunk Works referred to these concepts as ARCHANGEL-1, ARCHANGEL-2, etc., a carryover from the original ANGEL name used by the U-2 development project. These designs soon became simply A-1, A-2, etc.

Unlike the U-2, the government decided that a design competition would be beneficial, primarily as a risk-reduction tool. The CIA issued requirements to Lockheed and Convair, and both contractors submitted proposals during the summer of 1959, but on July 14, 1959, the CIA rejected both designs. Revised proposals were submitted on August 20, 1959. The two aircraft were generally similar in performance, and the Lockheed design was selected mainly due to cost. However, the selection panel expressed concern about the A-11's vulnerability to radar detection, and the CIA asked Skunk Works to reduce the design's radar cross-section. It was during this radar testing that the aircraft received its characteristic cobra-like appearance and became the A-12. Lockheed

The A-12 was the most streamlined of the Blackbird series; it was slightly shorter and lighter than the later SR-71, and also somewhat faster and higher flying. The A-12 suffered a disappointing operational career and flew only 29 operational missions, mostly over Southeast Asia, before it was retired. This was not the result of any shortcomings of the aircraft itself, but reflected political and fiscal pressures being felt by officials in Washington. *Lockheed Martin Skunk Works*

The only two-seat A-12 was the *Titanium Goose,* which some reports have referred to as the A-12B. This is an unlikely designation, given the unofficial status of A-12 to begin with. This was the only Blackbird that Kelly Johnson ever flew in. The *Goose* spent its entire career powered by the original J75 engines that did not provide sufficient power to reach Mach 3. Since the *Goose* was intended as a trainer, the lack of speed was not considered a serious drawback. *Lockheed Martin Skunk Works*

came up with a theory that a continuously curving airframe would be difficult to track because it would present few corner reflections or sharp angles from which radar pulses could reflect. This is, interestingly, exactly the opposite of the theory that later led to the straight-edged F-117. To further reduce radar reflections, Johnson canted the vertical stabilizers 15 degrees inward and fabricated them out of resin-impregnated high-temperature plastic.

OXCART: ". . . Obviously Right."

According to the specifications, OXCART was to be capable of Mach 3.2 (2,064 knots or 0.57 miles per second, which would make it slightly faster than a 0.30-caliber rifle bullet), have a range of 4,120 nautical miles, and reach altitudes of 84,500 to 97,500 feet. The new aircraft would thus be more than five times as fast as the U-2 and would go almost 3 miles higher. By mid-January 1960 the changes needed to reduce the RCS had led to a reduction in the aircraft's performance.

To overcome the reduction in performance, Lockheed proposed reducing the aircraft's weight by 1,000 pounds and increasing the fuel load by 2,000 pounds, making it possible to achieve the target altitude of 90,000 feet. Afterward, Johnson noted in the ARCHANGEL project log: "We have no performance margins left; so this project, instead of being 10 times as hard as anything we have done, is 12 times as hard. This matches the design number and is obviously right."

The Advanced Manned Interceptor program resulted in three YF-12A prototypes being built by Skunk Works. These aircraft were generally similar to the CIA A-12s (note the rear fuselage ends even with the trailing edge), but featured a revised forward fuselage that raised the pilot for a better view and added a large ASG-18 weapons system and three AIM-47 missiles. The chines were cut to prevent interference with the radar in the nose, and to provide mounting locations for a pair of infrared search and track sensors (removed by the time this photo was taken). *Lockheed Martin Skunk Works*

Designed with slide rules in the days before computers, the Blackbirds would fly at altitudes where the ambient air temperature was -70 degrees Fahrenheit. Despite this seemingly frigid environment, the nose of the aircraft would heat up to 800 degrees Fahrenheit, the windshield to over 600 degrees Fahrenheit, and the exhaust section behind the engines would reach over 1,200 degrees Fahrenheit.

On January 26, 1960, the CIA authorized the construction of 12 OXCART aircraft. The first A-12 was assembled and checked out at Burbank during January and February 1962. Since it could not safely or secretly be flown to Groom Lake, the entire fuselage, minus the wings, was loaded on a specially designed trailer and left Burbank on February 26, 1962. It arrived at "The Ranch" two days later.

Lockheed test pilot Louis Schalk took the A-12 for an unofficial first flight on April 25, 1962, and flew less than 2 miles at an altitude of about 20 feet. This "flight"

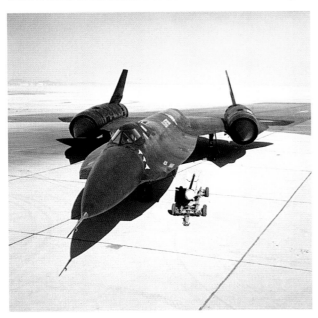

revealed several problems that were quickly repaired, and on April 26, Schalk made a 40-minute maiden flight. Kelly Johnson noted that this "was obviously a day for the A-12, in that 2 x 6 = 12." OXCART's "official" first flight took place on April 30, 1962, and it was witnessed by a number of CIA and air force representatives. On May 2, 1962, during the second test flight, OXCART broke the sound barrier, achieving a velocity of Mach 1.1.

The period devoted to OXCART flight tests was remarkably short considering the performance envelope that was being opened. By the end of 1963 there had been 573 flights totaling 765 hours by the nine aircraft in the inventory. On July 20, 1963, an A-12 first flew at Mach 3, and in November 1963 the design speed of Mach 3.2 was reached at 78,000 feet altitude. The longest sustained flight at design conditions occurred on February 3, 1964, and lasted 10 minutes at Mach 3.2 and 83,000 feet. By the end of 1964 there had been 1,160 flights, totaling 1,616 hours, with 9 hours maintained above Mach 3.

By November 20, 1965, the final validation flights prior to OXCART deployment were completed. During these tests, an A-12 achieved a maximum speed of Mach 3.29 at 90,000 feet, and sustained flight above Mach 3.2 for 74 minutes. On November 22, Johnson wrote to the CIA stating, "The time has come when the bird should leave its nest." Three years and seven months after its

The third YF-12A and a GAR-9 (AIM-47) air-to-air missile. This was after May 1965, as evidenced by the three record marks (white Blackbird silhouettes) on the nose. The YF-12 could carry three of these large missiles (there were four bays, but one was used to house additional fire control electronics), and scored an impressive record during tests. Seven missiles were fired at live targets at Eglin AFB, with six of the tests being considered successful. Five of the launches were made at speeds in excess of Mach 3.1 (the other two were at Mach 2.2) against either Ryan Q-2C or Boeing QB-47 drones. *Lockheed Martin Skunk Works*

The first D-21 drone was moved under the cover of darkness from its manufacturing area in Burbank's Building 82 to the Blackbird assembly area in Building 309/310 where it was mated to an M-21 (60-6940) mothership. In the designation scheme, "D" stood for daughter and "M" signified mother. The "21" was simply "12" reversed to prevent possible confusion with other A-12-related projects. At this point the drone was missing its outer wing panels, wing leading edges, and vertical stabilizer. The fuselage-to-wing fairing panels are missing on the M-21, showing some of the piping that ran through that area. *Lockheed Martin Skunk Works*

Externally the M-21 was virtually identical to the single-seat A-12 except for the small window in the second canopy and the launch pylon for the D-21. This photo was taken during the first captive-carry flight and shows the streamlined intake and exhaust covers that were originally fitted to the D-21. The first attempt to jettison these covers at high speed resulted in significant damage to the drone and the covers were deleted from all future flights. The additional drag was compensated for by running the drone's engine when needed. *Lockheed Martin Skunk Works*

Above: After the Blackbird-launched portion of the D-21 program was canceled, the Air Force modified two Boeing B-52H bombers to carry a pair of the drones. Since the ramjet engines needed to be boosted to supersonic speeds before they would work, a large booster was strapped under the drone. Two of the D-21Bs and their boosters weighed a total of 48,572 pounds—a heavy load even for a B-52H. Here the first D-21B is shown under the wing of one of the SENIOR BOWL B-52Hs. This drone was later lost when it was accidentally dropped from the wing of its B-52H. *Lockheed Martin Skunk Works*

first flight, OXCART was ready for operational use. It was now time to find work for the most advanced aircraft ever conceived and built.

Although OXCART had been designed to replace the U-2 as a strategic reconnaissance aircraft to overfly the Soviet Union, this use had become doubtful long before the A-12 was ready for operational use. The Powers U-2 incident in 1960 made the United States very reluctant to consider manned overflights of the Soviet Union. Presidents Eisenhower and Kennedy both stated publicly that the United States would not conduct such overflights. There was, however, a great deal of interest in deploying the aircraft to Southeast Asia where U.S. military activity was increasing.

On May 31, 1967, the first BLACK SHIELD mission departed Kadena AB in Okinawa and flew one pass over North Vietnam and another over the demilitarized zone. The mission was flown at Mach 3.1 and 80,000 feet, lasted 3 hours and 39 minutes, and photographed 70 of the 190 suspected surface-to-air sites and 9 other priority targets. During the next six weeks, there were seven more BLACK SHIELD missions.

Almost a decade had elapsed between the time when the concept for the OXCART aircraft was initially examined and the first operational A-12 mission.

Left: One of the D-21Bs just after being launched from a B-52. Under the power of its ramjet, the D-21 was capable of speeds in excess of Mach 3 at altitudes over 90,000 feet. The D-21 was perhaps the Blackbird's best-kept secret. The program existed for over 10 years before the public accidentally discovered it. Seventeen D-21s had been retired to Davis-Monthan AFB near Tucson, Arizona, and were dutifully covered by tarps to protect them from prying eyes. A chance windstorm blew some of the covers off on the same morning that a group of aviation enthusiasts were taking a tour of the storage area. Photos of the D-21s appeared in *Aviation Week* shortly thereafter. *Lockheed Martin Skunk Works*

The forward portion of each engine nacelle on the Blackbird was fixed, and did not swing upward with the outer wing panels. However, enough of the nacelle opened to allow complete access to the Pratt & Whitney J58 turbojet. Maintenance on the various inlet ramps and vents was accomplished by removing smaller panels around the nacelle. *Lockheed Martin Skunk Works*

After only 29 operational sorties, the most advanced aircraft ever built was retired. The abandonment of the OXCART did not result from any shortcomings of the aircraft, but happened because of fiscal pressures and competition between the reconnaissance programs of the CIA and the Air Force. In effect, OXCART was retired in preference to another Skunk Works aircraft—the SR-71.

Armed Oxcarts

Always seeking new opportunities, Johnson proposed a high-speed interceptor based on the A-12 design to the Air Force. Internally, the interceptor was referred to as the AF-12, and in late October 1960, the air force awarded a $1 million development contract to Lockheed under Project KEDLOCK.

The AF-12 was an A-12 modified with the AN/ASG-18 fire control system and three GAR-9 radar-guided air-to-air missiles from the stillborn North American XF-108 Rapier. The pilot's seat was raised for better visibility and a second seat (for the radar officer) added in a deeper, forward fuselage. In order to minimize distortion of the radar signals, the aerodynamic chines on the extreme nose had to be deleted and the radome lengthened. The modified chines also accommodated a pair of infrared search and track (IRST) sensors. The aft fuselage, wings, nacelles, and engines were identical to the CIA's A-12. A large folding ventral stabilizer was added under the aft fuselage and a small fixed ventral fin was added under each engine nacelle to restore the directional stability lost by cutting back the chines. This gave the AF-12 a very distinctive in-flight appearance. The Air Force ordered three AF-12s and negotiated with the CIA to use the seventh, eighth, and ninth A-12 airframes to speed the project along. By August 1962 the major elements of the first AF-12 were in the assembly jigs. The first AF-12 was trucked to Groom Lake in July 1963, and on August 7, Lockheed test pilot Jim Eastham made the aircraft's maiden flight.

On February 29, 1964, part of the Blackbird's security blanket was removed when President Johnson announced, "The United States has successfully developed an advanced experimental jet aircraft, the A-11, which has been tested in sustained flight at more than 2,000 miles per hour and at altitudes in excess of 70,000 feet. . . . The performance of the A-11 far exceeds that of any other aircraft in the world today. The development of this aircraft has been made possible by major advances in aircraft technology of great significance to both military and commercial applications. Several A-11 aircraft are now being flight-tested at Edwards AFB in California. . . . The A-11 aircraft now at Edwards AFB are undergoing extensive tests to determine their capabilities as long-range interceptors."

Of course this statement contained two nontruths. First, the reference to the A-11 was at Johnson's suggestion to mislead intelligence sources. Second, there were no Blackbirds of any description at Edwards AFB. Caught slightly off-guard by the president's announcement, two of the three AF-12s were quickly flown from Groom Lake to Edwards. In their haste to conceal the aircraft from public view, Schalk and Eastham made a direct approach and landed on Edwards' runway, taxied directly to the awaiting hangers, were pushed in tail first, and the doors were closed. The two AF-12s were still very hot from their dash from Groom Lake, and the heat set off the hanger's fire deluge system and covered the aircraft and ground crew in water. At the same time a proper Air Force designation (YF-12A) was assigned.

The various Blackbirds had routinely broken just about every speed record in existence, but nobody knew about it due to the security restrictions surrounding the programs. On August 12, 1964, the Air Force asked Lockheed to come up with a program to use the YF-12As to publicly break the records. The YF-12A was chosen primarily because it was the model with the greatest public exposure and it was much easier to explain why the Air Force needed a high-speed interceptor while it was more difficult to explain the CIA's need for an air force. The idea languished for some time, but finally on May 1, 1965, the first and third YF-12As were used to set several Class C Group III absolute records, including sustained altitude—80,257.65 feet (Col. Robert Stephens and Lt. Col. Daniel Andre); 15/25-kilometer closed course—2,070.101 miles per hour (Colonel Stephens and Lieutenant Colonel Andre); 500-kilometer closed course—1,643.042 miles per hour (Maj. Walter Daniel and Maj.

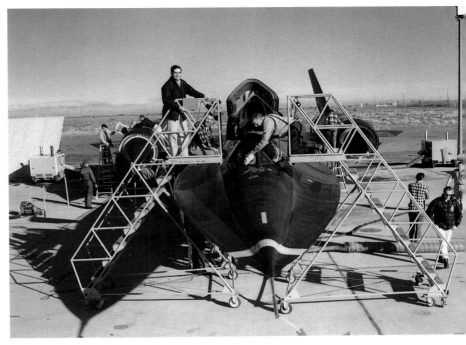

The white stripe around the nose distinguished the first SR-71, which was retained by Skunk Works as a test aircraft for its entire career. This aircraft was written off in an accident at Edwards AFB on January 10, 1967, when several tires failed during an antiskid braking test. The tires caught fire and it quickly spread to the rest of the aircraft. Lockheed test pilot Art Peterson survived. Two other SR-71s would be lost within two years due to landing gear failures, leading Skunk Works and the Air Force to develop more robust wheels and tires. *Lockheed Martin Skunk Works*

Noel Warner); and three 1,000 kilometer closed courses (without payload, with 1,000-kilogram payload, and with 2,000-kilogram payload)—1,688.891 miles per hour (Major Daniel and Capt. James Cooney).

The YF-12 program took a step closer to production on May 14, 1965, when the Air Force funded a $500,000

Unlike most aircraft, the Blackbird cruised with its afterburners lit, although this particular shot was taken as the aircraft accelerated away from a tanker. The shiny streaks under the fuselage are JP-7 leaks. This aircraft was NASA's SR-71B trainer. The three YF-12s and three trainers (SR-71B/C) were the only aircraft fitted with the ventral fins under the engine nacelles. *National Aeronautics and Space Administration via the Tony Landis Collection*

contract for engineering development of the follow-on F-12B. On January 5, 1968, the F-12B program was canceled in its entirety, and a similar fate befell the YF-12A program on February 1, 1968. The cancellation notice on the YF-12A program included orders to destroy all tooling for both the fighter and reconnaissance (A-12/SR-71) variants. The large assembly jigs were cut up and sold to local scrap dealers for seven cents per pound. However, many smaller tools and fixtures were placed in storage at nearby Norton AFB and supported the manufacture of spare parts for the SR-71s for many years.

Tagboard and Senior Bowl

When originally conceived in early 1958, the A-12's primary mission was to overfly the Soviet Union. When Francis Gary Powers was shot down on May 1, 1960, the rules changed. One of the many concessions made by President Eisenhower for the release of Powers was the immediate cessation of all manned overflights. The word "manned" was carefully stipulated because of the possibilities envisioned for future reconnaissance satellites. However, since the satellites were still several years away from operation, the CIA determined that a drone also fell outside the "manned" category.

On October 10, 1962, the CIA authorized Lockheed to study a drone code-named TAGBOARD specifically created to overfly the Soviet Union and China. No

detailed requirements appear to have been issued, and Johnson was free to develop what he felt was necessary.

Because of the complexities of turbojet engines and their associated intakes, a Marquardt ramjet was selected to power the new aircraft. This was much the same technology proven by Skunk Works during the X-7 project 10 years earlier. Since ramjet engines do not function at low speeds, a modified two-seat A-12 (designated M-21) was selected as a launch platform. The drone was originally known within Skunk Works as the Q-12. As work progressed with the project, it was given the D-21 designation.

Unlike the original A-12s, the M-21 carried a back seat for the launch control officer who used a periscope to monitor the "daughter." A dorsal-mounted pylon carried the D-21 and aerodynamic considerations required that the M-21 "push over" during launch instead of flying straight and level as originally intended, a choice that was later regretted. Only 6 inches of clearance existed between the D-21's wingtips and the top of the M-21's vertical stabilizers.

The first captive-carry flight occurred on December 22, 1964, on the same day the first SR-71 made its maiden flight. The first successful launch from an M-21 was finally made on March 5, 1966, over the Pacific Ocean somewhere between Port Mugu and Vandenberg AFB with the drone having only 25 percent of its design fuel load. A launch with a 50 percent fuel load was made on April 27, 1966, and a full fuel launch was made on June 16, 1966.

During the fourth launch flight on July 30, 1966, the D-21 impacted the M-21 at Mach 3.25, and destroyed the mothership's right rudder, right engine nacelle, and most of the outer wing panel. The Blackbird tumbled out of control into the Pacific. Both Bill Park and Ray Torick successfully ejected, but Torick's pressure suit was torn during the ejection and filled with water immediately upon landing. Torick drowned before rescue teams could arrive on the scene.

Each of the SR-71s had its own private hanger at Beale AFB, California. All maintenance was performed in the hanger, and the entire preflight check was done inside. Both the front and rear of the hanger opened to allow the engines to be started while under the protective roof of the hanger. Each of the A-12s had enjoyed similar hangers at Groom Lake, and other hangers were built at the Kadena AB, Okinawa, and RAF Mildenhall, United Kingdom, operating locations. *Lockheed Martin Skunk Works photo by Eric Schulzinger*

A Dark Day for Skunk Works

The M-21-launch portion of TAGBOARD was terminated the following month. Johnson had already initiated preliminary studies of using a rocket to accelerate the D-21 to speed after launch from a larger aircraft. The remaining D-21 drones were modified for launch from Boeing B-52Hs and redesignated D-21B under Project SENIOR BOWL. Two B-52Hs were modified and conducted with a total of 17 launches and 4 operational missions prior to the program being terminated on July 23, 1971.

The existence of the D-21 was also the Blackbird's best-kept secret. It existed for over 10 years and had been removed from service before the public accidentally discovered it. Seventeen D-21s had been retired to Davis-Monthan AFB near Tucson, Arizona, and dutifully covered by tarps to protect them from prying eyes. A windstorm blew some of the covers off the drones on the same morning that a group of aviation enthusiasts were taking a tour of the storage area. Photographs of the D-21s appeared in *Aviation Week* shortly thereafter.

The Senior Crown

In December 1962 the Air Force ordered 6 Blackbirds under the SENIOR CROWN contract, and added 25 more in August 1963. Internally Lockheed referred to the new aircraft as the R-12. It was a reconfigured A-12 that was slightly longer and heavier to accommodate different reconnaissance systems and a second crew member. The "Q" bay, which housed the A-12's very capable camera system, became the cockpit for the reconnaissance systems officer (RSO), and the sensor systems moved into bays in the same location as the missiles on the YF-12As. The Air Force aircraft were capable of using side-looking radar in addition to several different cameras, and also incorporated the ability to collect signal intelligence (SIGINT). The additional weight of all

This was the final operational paint scheme for the SR-71s with no national markings and only small red tail codes and serial numbers on the vertical stabilizer. Fuel is being vented from the extreme rear fuselage. The SR-71 did not use conventional rudders. Instead, the entire upper portion of each vertical stabilizer rotated to provide a substantial area that was seldom deflected more than a few degrees. *Lockheed Martin Skunk Works*

The surviving SR-71B trainer is now operated by NASA from the Dryden Flight Research Center at Edwards, California. Other than having a white NASA stripe painted on the vertical stabilizer along with the NASA aircraft number, very little has changed. The aircraft still does not sport national insignia or many markings. The raised second cockpit allows an instructor some measure of forward visibility during training missions. *National Aeronautics and Space Administration*

this equipment resulted in a slower maximum speed and a lower operating ceiling.

The Air Force designated the aircraft RS-71 following the stillborn RS-70 version of the XB-70 strategic bomber. The process of making public the various versions of the Blackbird continued on July 25, 1964, when President Johnson revealed the existence of a new reconnaissance aircraft that he called the "SR-71" instead of "RS-71." Deciding that renaming the aircraft was easier than correcting the president, the air force invented a new category ("strategic reconnaissance") to explain the SR-71's designation.

In the early morning darkness of October 29, 1964, the first SR-71 departed Burbank aboard one of the same specially developed trailers used by all other Blackbirds. Unlike the A-12 and YF-12s before it, the SR-71 would make its first flight from Air Force Plant 42 in Palmdale, California, only 50 miles from Burbank. All of the earlier aircraft had gone to Groom Lake for their first flights. The aircraft's maiden flight took place on December 22, 1964, with Lockheed test pilot Robert J. Gilliland at the controls and an empty back seat. The flight lasted just over an hour, and the SR-71 attained a maximum speed of slightly over 1,000 miles per hour. Not bad for a first flight!

Just over a year later on January 7, 1966, the air force took delivery of its first Blackbird, a SR-71B trainer, at Beale AFB, California. All 31 of the original SR-71s would be delivered by the end of 1967. The 32nd aircraft, the sole SR-71C, would be assembled later after the second SR-71B trainer was lost in an accident on January 11, 1968.

Without aerial refueling, the range of the SR-71 was limited to approximately 2,000 miles at operational speeds. Multiple aerial refuelings could extend the range of the aircraft past the practical limit of the crew's endurance, and missions of 12,000 miles were not uncommon. A total of 35 Boeing Stratotankers were modified to the KC-135Q configuration used by the Blackbirds.

Retirement

By the mid-1980s there was increasing pressure to retire the last of the Blackbirds. The official reason was that the aircraft was getting too old to maintain and too expensive to operate. Amongst the general public it was widely believed that the Blackbird was being retired because a superior replacement (Aurora) was entering service, although there is still no conclusive evidence of such a vehicle.

The FY90 defense appropriations request simply did not contain funding for the SR-71. A great deal of lobbying occurred on each side of the debate, but in the end, no funds were forthcoming. The last operational training sortie was flown on November 7, 1989—21 years, 7 months, and 17 days after the first SR-71 operational sortie.

On December 20, 1989, an SR-71A made a pass down the Burbank runway to honor all those who worked in designing and producing the fastest air-breathing piloted aircraft in the world. Johnson, who had been long retired and was gravely ill, was there to watch. On March 6, 1990, nearly two months after the SR-71 was officially retired from the air force, the BIG SAFARI project office used an SR-71A to set four international speed records while it was being delivered to the Smithsonian National Air and Space Museum at Dulles International Airport, Washington, D.C. The aircraft flew coast-to-coast (2,404 miles) in 67 minutes and 54 seconds, and averaged 2,124 miles per hour.

Kelly Johnson would pass away nine months later, on December 21, 1990. He will forever be a legend, like the aircraft he created.

Less than a year after the SR-71s were retired, it became apparent just how wrong the decision was to retire them. When Operation DESERT SHIELD began, Gen. Norman Schwarzkopf was reported to have asked for SR-71s to be reactivated for use in gathering near-real-time reconnaissance over Iraq and Kuwait. The Air Force asked Skunk Works how long it would take to reactivate one or more of the SR-71As in storage at Plant 42. Lockheed responded that a single aircraft could be operational within two weeks and a second aircraft 30 days later. The Air Force declined the opportunity.

On September 19, 1994, Congress authorized $100 million and ordered the Air Force to bring three SR-71s out of storage. The air force's BIG SAFARI project office managed the project that saw the first of the reactivated SR-71As fly its initial sortie on April 26, 1995. The second reactivated SR-71A made its first flight on August 28, 1995, and both aircraft were equipped with a new satellite data link to provide near-real-time transmission of intelligence data. The original government estimate for reactivating and updating two aircraft was $100 million, and the final cost was somewhat less than $72 million; another tribute to Skunk Works' efficiency.

The SR-71 program was grounded again in 1996 because the Air Force said specific funding was not authorized. Congress again authorized the funds, but in October 1997 President Bill Clinton used the line-item veto to zero the $39 million for the SR-71. In June 1998 the Supreme Court ruled the line-item veto unconstitutional, sending the SR-71 back into limbo. Finally, in September 1998 the Air Force asked that the funds be redistributed, and the SR-71 was permanently retired. The Air Force wasted little time in disposing of the remaining Blackbird assets and left two NASA aircraft as the last flyable Blackbirds.

Even as complex and sophisticated as the Blackbird was, it went 17 straight years without an accident. Nevertheless, 6 of the 15 OXCARTs built were written off, as were 2 of the 3 YF-12As. Over the 30 years that the SR-71 flew for the Air Force, 11 were lost—4 of the 6 test aircraft, the second SR-71B, and 6 operational SR-71As. None were lost to enemy action. All of the remaining Blackbirds are in museums except for a couple of SR-71s and some D-21 drones retained by NASA.

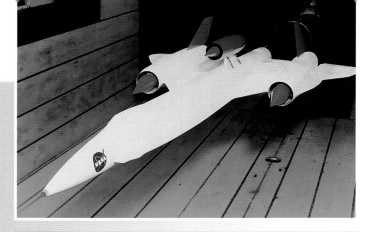

NASA's First Blackbirds

NASA's involvement with the Blackbird began in earnest during 1967. NASA wanted an instrumented SR-71A to use for its own research, but after that failed, NASA was willing to install an instrument package on one of the SR-71A test aircraft. The Air Force declined, but offered NASA the use of two YF-12As (60-6935 and -6936) then in storage at Edwards. A team from the Air Defense Command would be made available for maintenance and logistics support. A memorandum of understanding was signed June 5, 1969, followed by a public announcement on July 18.

The other YF-12A (60-6936) had just embarked on its joint NASA–Air Force research program when it crashed. During a flight on June 24, 1971, the Blackbird experienced fatigue failure of a fuel line, resulting in a fire in the right engine nacelle. Lt. Col. Ronald J. Layton and Maj. Billy A. Curtis debated whether they could land the burning Blackbird but they wisely decided to eject from the aircraft. The YF-12A crashed in the desert near Edwards' runway and the remains were later moved to a commercial scrap yard in nearby Rosamond.

NASA had wanted to add a third aircraft to the YF-12A test program solely for propulsion tests. A month after the loss of 60-6936, the Air Force made the second SR-71 (64-17951) available to NASA. Because the SR-71 program was still shrouded in secrecy, this aircraft was fictitiously designated YF-12C and carried the equally fictitious serial number 60-6937 (this serial number was also used by an A-12). On May 24, 1972, the YF-12C made its first NASA flight. The NASA Blackbirds flew an average of once a week, and program expenses averaged $3.1 million per year.

Flight tests of the YF-12s furnished rather interesting data. For example, at Mach 3, half of the aircraft's total drag came from simply venting air overboard through the inlet bypass doors. Also, a gray area was discovered between stability and control. Inlet components were almost as effective as elevons and rudders in influencing aircraft motion at high speeds. Inlet spike motion and bypass door operation could alter the aircraft's flight path under some conditions. The airflow dumped overboard through the inlet louvers entered a "stagnation area" just ahead of the louvers and actually flowed forward along the outside of the nacelle for a brief distance before mixing with the Mach 3 air stream and moving aft.

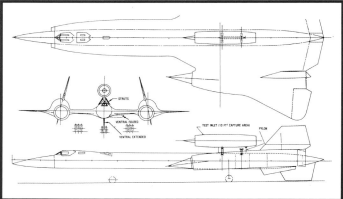

High-performance inlet systems are very sensitive to many factors that are difficult to simulate during wind tunnel testing of small-scale models. NASA investigated using their YF-12As to carry a test version of a supersonic inlet in support of the supersonic transport (SST) program. This configuration was tested in wind tunnels, but the SST program was cancelled and the concept was never built or flown. *National Aeronautics and Space Administration*

By the early part of 1977, the NASA YF-12s had completed more than 175 flights with a good percentage at or above Mach 3. But the cost of flying the two high-performance aircraft became too great a burden for NASA, and in the spring of 1977, NASA decided to retire the YF-12A and to return the YF-12C to the Air Force. The YF-12C was finally returned on October 27, 1978, and put into storage along with the nine remaining A-12s at Plant 42. The sole remaining YF-12A made its 146th and final flight to the Air Force Museum on November 7, 1979, and the world's only Mach 3 fighter program came to an end.

The 12 single-seat A-12s accumulated slightly over 3,727 hours of flight time during 2,189 flights. The lone two-seat trainer added another 1,076 hours in 614 flights. This underpowered two-seater, not capable of Mach 3 flight, was the only Blackbird that Kelly Johnson ever flew in.

The SR-71's record includes a total of 53,490 flight hours during 17,300 missions. This includes 11,008 hours that were accumulated during 3,551 operational reconnaissance missions over North Korea, North Vietnam, the Middle East, South Africa, Cuba, Nicaragua, Iran, Libya, and the Falkland Islands. More than 11,675 of these hours, including 2,752 during actual operations, were spent above Mach 3. Perhaps more than any other aircraft, the Blackbirds showed the genius of Johnson and Skunk Works.

Maximum Performance

The performance potential of the Blackbird is only now becoming well understood. The SR-71 was intended for flight at altitudes approaching 85,000 feet, with sustained cruising speeds approaching Mach 3.2. The smaller and lighter A-12 could better each of these by a small margin. During its operational career, the SR-71 rarely exceeded these design speed or altitude limits. Studies have been conducted by Lockheed and NASA that show speeds in excess of Mach 3.5 could be attained for 10 to 15 minutes. The studies indicated that increasing the maximum speed to Mach 3.4 would not require any significant modifications to the aircraft, but for sustained flight between Mach 3.4 and Mach 3.5, the inlet hydraulic lines and actuators would need to be better insulated to protect them from the additional heat. NASA had planned to conduct an envelope expansion program for the SR-71, but ever tightening budgets led to these plans being canceled in the early 1990s. The only structural limitation related to speed above Mach 3.5 is an absolute limit of 420 knots equivalent air speed (KEAS), set by inlet duct pressures and temperatures which exceed acceptable values. Other factors that limit speed above Mach 3.5 are inlet capture area and excessive engine compressor inlet temperature (CIT).

One of the NASA studies also addressed achieving higher-altitude flight. The results indicated that a "zoom climb" profile would allow reaching 95,000 feet for a short time with an aircraft gross weight of approximately 85,000 pounds. The aircraft would be accelerated from Mach 3.2 to Mach 3.5 at an altitude of 80,000 feet, then zoomed to 95,000 feet, with speed decaying back to approximately Mach 3.2. The aircraft would subsequently settle back to an altitude of 84,000 feet. Factors which limit sustained flight at altitudes above 85,000 feet are wing area and total thrust. It would be possible to replace the outer wing panels with larger ones to provide additional wing surface area and allow sustained flight above 85,000 feet.

Three

Almost every aspect of the F-117A received attention to reduce its radar signature. This is most obvious with the faceting of the canopy and FLIR openings. Similar efforts were made on the landing gear doors, weapons bay doors, and most maintenance panels. Every angle is precisely aligned to reflect radar away from the receiver, and allows the F-117 to slip through undetected. *Lockheed Martin Skunk Works*

>> Stealth Fighters—
THE F-117 AND YF-22

The Beginning of Stealth

By the late 1950s, operational U-2 missions were being flown on a routine basis, and the ability of the Soviets to track the U-2 was alarming to all concerned. Skunk Works began investigating means to reduce the U-2's radar signature, and Johnson developed various concepts, some of which were quite fantastic and of questionable value. Perhaps the most bizarre was one to string wires of various lengths between the fuselage, wings, and tail of the U-2 in order to scatter the radar energy in different directions. The concept was intended to counter low-frequency 70MHz surveillance radars. The wires would be mounted a quarter-wavelength away from the leading and trailing edges of the wing and tail surfaces so that the return from the wire would ideally be canceled out by the return from the surface leading edge, and would be 180 degreees out of phase with each other. In a speech given at the 1975 Radar Camouflage Symposium, Johnson said: "The aircraft so equipped was flight tested with negligible results in reduction of radar cross-section together with the expected adverse aerodynamic effects."

The idea that was finally chosen for more extensive flight testing involved wrapping the entire airframe with a metallic grid known as SALISBURY SCREEN which was covered by a microwave absorbent ECHOSORB coating made of foam rubber, now called radar-absorbing material (RAM). The resulting aircraft were often referred to as Dirty Birds, and were universally disliked by pilots for their degraded handling qualities. However, none of the materials tested proved effective across the entire spectrum of Soviet radar frequencies, and all extracted a considerable penalty on aircraft performance. The coatings also prevented the dissipation of heat from the engine through the aircraft skin. During a Dirty

The First Stealth Efforts

When operational U-2 missions began being flown on a routine basis, the ability of the Soviets to track the aircraft was alarming to all concerned. Skunk Works began investigating means to reduce the U-2's radar signature, and Kelly Johnson developed various concepts, some of which were quite fantastic and of questionable value. Perhaps the most bizarre idea was to string wires of various lengths between the fuselage, wings, and tail in order to scatter the radar energy in different directions. The idea that was finally flight-tested involved wrapping the entire airframe with a metallic grid known as SALISBURY SCREEN, which was covered by a microwave absorbent ECHOSORB coating made of foam rubber. The resulting aircraft were often referred to as Dirty Birds, and were almost universally disliked by pilots for their degraded handling qualities. However, none of the materials proved effective across the entire spectrum of Soviet radar frequencies, and all extracted a considerable penalty on aircraft performance. The coatings also prevented the dissipation of heat from the engine through the aircraft skin. During a Dirty Bird test flight with the U-2 prototype (Article 341), Bob Sieker experienced a flameout at 72,000 feet due to a heat buildup caused by the foam coating. Unfortunately Sieker's pressure suit faceplate failed, and he suffocated before the U-2 crashed in the desert.

Further analysis by Johnson indicated that the only effective way of producing a smaller RCS was to design an aircraft with that objective from the beginning. This objective gave birth to the A-12/SR-71 program. About the only thing that could be done for the U-2 was to paint it in such a way as to provide a small measure against being visually detected by fighters attempting to intercept during an over-flight. Originally, all air force U-2s were left in their natural metal finish. During 1961 and 1962 they were repainted in a high-gloss light

gray. Various schemes, including polka dots and zebra stripes, were flight-tested over Edwards, but none proved terribly effective. The CIA decided to paint their aircraft a very dark "midnight blue" since it would blend into the dark sky that is prevalent at high altitude, and the air force followed in 1964. In many photographs this particular shade of blue takes on an almost glossy sheen. In 1965 the Air Force introduced the BLACK VELVET paint scheme that used an extremely flat black paint, and by 1966 all air force and CIA aircraft had been repainted.

Two J57 engines are visible in the foreground, and the small workstands used to support the wingtips during maintenance are visible on the closest aircraft. Although difficult to notice, the aircraft in the right front is configured as a Dirty Bird with an ECHOSORB radar-absorbing coating over the entire exterior. This coating was not terribly effective and prevented heat transfer from the airframe, which caused at least one in-flight accident. The NACA insignia on the vertical stabilizer in the background was a ruse often employed during early U-2 operations. *Lockheed Martin Skunk Works*

Bird test flight with the U-2 prototype, Bob Sieker experienced a flameout at 72,000 feet due to heat buildup caused by the foam coating. Unfortunately Sieker's pressure suit faceplate failed and he suffocated before the U-2 crashed in the desert.

The A-12 was the first serious attempt to build an operational aircraft with a reduced RCS. In comparison to other aircraft of its era, the A-12 was very successful. However, technology was progressing rapidly, and the advent of more capable signal processing computers would quickly overcome whatever advantage the A-12 might have had when it was developed. The ultimate development of the basic A-12 shape, the D-21 drone, incorporated even more RAM into the design and was considered the "stealthiest" aircraft of its era even though the term still did not exist at the time.

In 1966 the Teledyne Ryan AQM-91A Compass Arrow high-altitude reconnaissance drone became the next serious attempt to reduce an aircraft's RCS. The vertical stabilizers and sides of the fuselage were canted inward to eliminate specular reflections from the side aspect or below the horizontal plane. The engine inlet was located above the fuselage and lined with RAM. The exhaust nozzle was located on top of the fuselage to obscure it from below, and cooling air was mixed with the exhaust to lower the infared signature. RAM was also applied to the wing leading edge and to some fuselage panels near the wing junction. Although the design was moderately successful at reducing the drone's RCS, it also revealed that a conventional wing-body design would probably never truly be "stealthy."

Have Blue—DARPA Discovers Stealth

In 1974 the Defense Advanced Research Projects Agency (DARPA) issued $100,000 contracts to McDonnell Douglas and Northrop to study what RCS reduction was necessary to ensure the survival of an aircraft in a high-threat environment. Hughes Aircraft, which contrary to its name did not build aircraft but rather the

An early Have Blue model undergoing a test in Lockheed's Rye Canyon anachoic chamber. Note that the trailing edge of the wings does not sweep forward as severely as the final design. There is a noticeable diamond shape leading to a somewhat triangular cross-section on the faceting on the outside of the vertical stabilizers. *Lockheed Martin Skunk Works*

radar systems that equipped them, was also funded to evaluate various aspects of the study. These initial studies were classified "confidential," the lowest of the three traditional security levels (confidential, secret, and top secret). The magnitude of the problem was large. In order to reduce the detection range by a factor of 10, the RCS of the target has to be reduced by a factor of 10,000. Previous efforts had managed RCS reductions of less than 50 percent—barely noticeable in real terms. When Johnson found out about the studies, he approached the CIA for permission to brief DARPA on

The second HAVE BLUE demonstrator during initial ground testing at Burbank. Following these tests, the aircraft was partially disassembled and moved to Groom Lake on the night of November 16, 1977. The rudders appear to be faceted, but unlike the F-117A, there is no particular faceting around the canopy or landing gear doors. *Lockheed Martin Skunk Works*

some of the RCS-reduction techniques tried on the U-2 and A-12. Since the aircraft were public knowledge by this time, the CIA voiced no particular objections, and DARPA soon included Lockheed in the studies.

McDonnell Douglas was the first to publish a report detailing the RCS value necessary to defeat most surveillance radars. These values were later validated independently by Hughes. This was not surprising since McDonnell Douglas had already conducted some classified research for the Office of Naval Research (ONR) during 1973 on a "Quiet Attack" aircraft. This was an early attempt to design a stealth aircraft, although in this case the term was not limited to radar evading technology. The visual signature of the Quiet Attack aircraft was reduced by the use of airframe-mounted Yehudi Lights that intended to mimic ambient lighting, and the infrared signature was reduced through the use of a novel exhaust nozzle for the single turbojet engine. The

The first F-117A wore a three-color desert scheme paint job for its first 10 flights. This aircraft's vertical stabilizers are smaller than usual, and the canopy is not faceted. Larger vertical surfaces were fitted during a modification period after the 10th flight. A large boom with alpha and beta vanes is mounted on the centerline of the extreme nose. Only three pilots flew the aircraft during these first 10 flights—Harold C. Farley (Hal), Skip Anderson, and Dave Furguson. *U.S. Air Force*

The first F-117A is lifted out of the final assembly jig. This is the almost-complete fuselage structure. There are also an aft fuselage, extreme nose, wings, and vertical stabilizers that need to be added. There are very few access panels on this part of the fuselage, although the large cutouts for the air intakes can be seen under and behind the cockpit area. *Lockheed Martin Skunk Works*

aircraft was vaguely reminiscent of the P-80 in plain view, but incorporated a curved outline, a blended wing-body, and a butterfly-like empennage. RAM was used in some areas to further reduce the radar signature.

The constantly curving airframe, using much the same logic that Lockheed had used on the A-12, significantly reduced the RCS, but the fact that a small edge was always perpendicular to the incoming radar ensured that a small return was always generated. McDonnell Douglas intended to use active jamming to counter the small perpendicular return, and the navy considered this a fair tradeoff, but in the end the aircraft was never built. DARPA was less interested in visual signature reduction and flatly rejected the use of active jamming.

Lockheed and Northrop took a different approach. Lockheed's design was based on the results of some very obscure formulae that had originally been devised by Scotsman James Clark Maxwell and German Arnold Johannes Sommerfield in the early 1900s to predict the way any given geometric shape would reflect microwave energy. The formulae went largely unnoticed until 1962 when Piotr Ufimstev, chief scientist at the Moscow Institute of Radio Engineering, used them as the basis for an

All 60 F-117As were manufactured by Skunk Works in Burbank's Building 309/310. The assembly line was fairly simple and unautomated—fitting for a program that knows it will be producing a very small number of aircraft. The aft fuselage is being attached in the extreme lower left corner, and mid-fuselage sections are being built up in the center row. *Lockheed Martin Skunk Works*

Does anybody know the way to Groom Lake? A partially disassembled F-117A will barely fit inside a Lockheed C-5 Galaxy transport, and this was the way most of the F-117As were initially transported to the test facility at Groom Lake. Although the aircraft were wrapped in tarps, most operations were still conducted at night to keep prying eyes from discerning what was happening. *Lockheed Martin Skunk Works*

openly published paper on calculating the radar return of a two-dimensional object. Although the paper was seemingly ignored by Soviet aircraft designers, Denys Overholster at Skunk Works decided that it offered a way to assist in designing a low-RCS aircraft.

Although the formulae were capable of predicting the effects for constantly curving structures, the computers at the time could not handle the enormous number of calculations necessary within a reasonable period of time. Overholster decided to break down the aircraft into a series of flat panels since the computers could handle a relatively small number of calculations. This gave birth to the multifaceted design for the HAVE BLUE and F-117. Within a few years there had been significant

advances in computer technology that allowed Northrop and McDonnell Douglas to use continuously curving designs for the B-2 and navy's A-12 attack aircraft.

Skunk Works was primarily concerned with reducing the head-on RCS in order to minimize the possibility of detection while flying to a target. The individual surfaces and edges were oriented in such a way that they reflected microwave energy into narrow beams away from the original source. If each small flat surface could be angled differently so that it would reflect energy away from the transmitter, then the overall radar signature of the entire aircraft should be quite small.

After a great deal of experimentation, Lockheed determined that the optimum shape for the aircraft was a

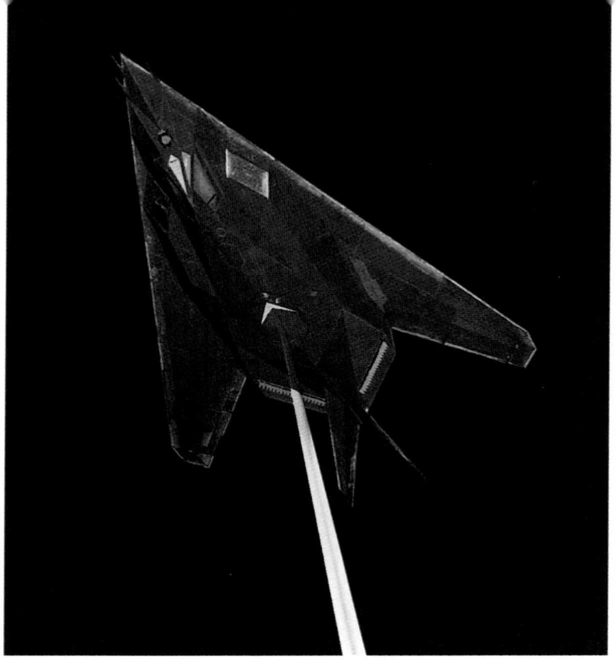

A full-scale SENIOR TREND was also tested on the Lockheed RCS measurement range at Helendale, California. Most of the testing was conducted at night to minimize the chances of the aircraft being seen by uncleared personnel and passing satellites. The Helendale facility is extremely sophisticated, and the pole the aircraft is mounted on can be retracted into an underground cavern when it is not being actively tested. *Lockheed Martin Skunk Works*

From almost any angle, the F-117A has a bizarre appearance. The small blade antenna in the top of the fuselage is retractable (as are several under the fuselage) in order to preserve the stealth characteristics of the aircraft. A small radar reflector can be seen just behind the national insignia. When operating in stealth mode (antennas retracted and no radar reflectors installed), the aircraft can still communicate with friendly forces by a secure low-probability-of-intercept (LPI) system that uses upward-facing antennas just behind the cockpit. This system links the F-117A pilot, via burst transmissions and frequency-hopping techniques, to satellites, AWACS, and U-2s, to allow real-time strike information to be discussed even during stealth operations. *Lockheed Martin Skunk Works photo by Judson Brohmer*

beveled diamond, which was quickly dubbed the "Hopeless Diamond" since it was aerodynamically impossible to fly. Insiders have reported that the Hopeless Diamond had an RCS 1,000 times less than the D-21, but the world's least visible aircraft was worthless if it could not fly. Lockheed set about making modifications to the design such as slimming down the outer portions of the aft edges to become small wings, creating the notched delta planform later used on the HAVE BLUE demonstrators. Two vertical stabilizers, severely canted inward to the point that their tips almost touched, were added to improve directional stability.

On November 1, 1975, Lockheed and Northrop were selected for Phase I of the Experimental Survivable Testbed (XST) program. This would involve building full-scale models of their designs for testing at a radar measuring facility, designing an actual flight vehicle, flight control simulation, and wind tunnel testing. The final tests revealed that Lockheed's design enjoyed a

A flight of stealth fighters shows the general lack of markings used by the type. Other than small national insignia, the only markings are unit badges behind the intakes, and tail codes on the vertical stabilizers. *Lockheed Martin Skunk Works photo by Judson Brohmer*

slight edge over the Northrop design from most directions. In itself it was probably not enough to swing the decision, but combined with Skunk Works' known track record with "black" projects and their experience with advanced composite materials, there was consensus that Lockheed was most likely to succeed. In April 1976 Lockheed was declared the winner of Phase I and was awarded a $19.2-million Phase II contract to manufacture two HAVE BLUE demonstrators. In the end, HAVE BLUE would cost a total of $43 million—Lockheed provided $10.4 million of their own funds, and the government would pay the rest.

Program management for Phase II was transferred from DARPA to the Air Force, which promptly imposed a "special access required" classification on the program to ensure that very little of the project would be known outside of the people directly involved. Even budget requests would be hidden in such a manner that the majority of Congress and the Office of Management and Budget did not know the HAVE BLUE demonstrators were being developed. Special access is above and beyond the normal three-tier classification levels, and essentially these programs do not exist except to a very few people.

Northrop's efforts were seen to have promise and DARPA subsequently awarded Northrop a contract to design a Battlefield Surveillance Aircraft, Experimental (BSAX) that led directly to the TACIT BLUE stealth surveillance prototype. This aircraft provided valuable data for the B-2 program, and managed to remain completely unknown until the aircraft was turned over to the Air Force Museum in 1996.

Have Blue

The word *demonstrator* is important. HAVE BLUE was never intended to produce an operational aircraft, or even a true prototype. The project was meant simply to demonstrate the concept of radically altering an aircraft's shape to achieve a significant reduction in RCS. A second objective was to prove the aircraft could fly.

The modified Hopeless Diamond design served as a basis for the HAVE BLUE demonstrators. Engine intakes were located on top of the shape and covered with metal mesh grids that appeared solid to microwave energy. By November 1977 the first aircraft had been completed and powered up inside the hanger at Burbank where it was built. In order to run the engines as final checks, the aircraft was taken outside the night of November 4 and surrounded by large trucks to shield it from any potential prying eyes. The aircraft was then partially disassembled, loaded into a C-5A on November 16, and transported to the CIA's old U-2 base at Groom Lake. It had only been 20 months since Lockheed had been awarded the HAVE BLUE contract.

The HAVE BLUE aircraft made its maiden flight on December 1, 1977, and was piloted by William M. "Bill"

Park. Flight tests of the HAVE BLUE went fairly smoothly, but on May 4, 1978, the first aircraft landed excessively hard and jammed the right main landing gear in a semi-retracted position. Park pulled the aircraft back into the air, and tried to shake the gear back down. After his third attempt failed, he took the aircraft up to 10,000 feet and ejected. The aircraft was written off, and Park was forced to retire from flying as a result of injuries suffered during the ejection.

The second HAVE BLUE made its maiden flight on July 20, 1978, with Maj. Norman "Ken" Dyson at the controls. The aircraft proved to be essentially unde-tectable by all U.S. airborne radars except for the Boeing E-3 AWACS, which could only acquire the aircraft at short ranges. Most ground-based missile tracking radars could detect the HAVE BLUE only after it was well inside the minimum range for the surface-to-air missiles with which they were associated. It was discovered that the best tactic to avoid radar detection was to approach the radar site head-on, presenting the HAVE BLUE's small nose-on signature.

Originally the HAVE BLUE program had scheduled 55 flights for the second aircraft, but on July 11, 1979, during its 52nd test flight, the aircraft suffered a double hydraulic failure and fire. Major Dyson successfully ejected and was not injured, but the aircraft was a total loss. Since the project was winding down in any case, the loss of the aircraft had minimal impact. The wreckage of both HAVE BLUEs was subsequently buried on the Groom Lake reservation.

The SENIOR TREND—The Birth of the Nighthawk

On November 16, 1977, Skunk Works was awarded a full-scale development contract under the project SENIOR TREND. Initially based on the HAVE BLUE config-uration, SENIOR TREND rapidly diverged in several impor-tant ways. First, the wing sweep was reduced to solve some of the center-of-gravity problems experienced dur-

A trio of F-117As prepares to launch. The stealth fighter is not a particularly small aircraft, and the main wing and fuselage stand almost 6 feet above the pavement. *Lockheed Martin Skunk Works photo by Denny Lombard*

ing flight tests of the HAVE BLUE design, and the forward fuselage was shortened to allow the pilot and planned sensors to have a better view over the nose. The most visible change was the vertical stabilizers that canted outboard from the centerline instead of canting inboard from the outer parts of the body.

In an effort to eliminate potential security leaks and to save time and money, Lockheed elected to use as many already available components as possible. The engine was a non-afterburning version of the General Electric F404 used by the F/A-18. The heads-up display (HUD), ejection seat, control column, and minor cock-pit equipment also came from the F/A-18. The flight control computers were from the F-16 program, while the landing gear was from the F-15. The inertial naviga-tion system came from stocks maintained for the B-52.

The positioning of the F-117A cockpit makes the use of a workstand pretty much mandatory since the aircraft does not have a built-in ladder. In an unusual bit of field engineering, technicians and pilots discovered that the articulating ladders sold in many home improvement shops could be set up in such a way as to provide easy access to the cockpit without damaging the RAM on the outside of the aircraft. These ladders are readily available and inexpensive, and have become the standard way to gain access to the F-117 when operating from austere field sites. *Lockheed Martin Skunk Works*

The forward-looking infrared (FLIR) equipment was also off the shelf, from some of the more interesting OV-10D derivatives (and also used on some P-3 aircraft). It was possible for Lockheed and the Air Force to simply procure these parts from available inventory or to order more as spare parts, and nobody was the wiser. Combined with a relatively small and dedicated workforce, this helped ensure the SENIOR TREND would remain a secret. The initial order was for 5 full-scale development (FSD) aircraft, although the air force quickly established a requirement for 20 production versions. Eventually 59 aircraft would be ordered to equip two silver bullet squadrons.

When SENIOR TREND had begun, it was expected that the first aircraft would fly in July 1980, but Lockheed ran into difficulties assembling the aircraft, and the program ran about a year behind schedule. In May 1981 the first SENIOR TREND was finally shipped to Groom Lake inside a C-5A, much like the HAVE BLUEs before it. On June 18, 1981, Harold "Hal" Farley, Jr. took the first SENIOR TREND on its maiden flight. All of the SENIOR TREND aircraft were manufactured at Burbank and transported to either Groom Lake or Tonopah in C-5s where they were reassembled and flown for the first time. No first flights were made from Burbank.

The radar signature has been reported as between 0.1 and 0.01 square meters. By comparison, an F-4 had a front RCS of over 6 square meters. In theory this allows the aircraft to get 90 percent closer to a given radar without being detected than was possible with the F-4.

Skunk Works manufactured the first nine prototype AGM-158 Joint Air-to-Surface Standoff Missiles (JASSM) for Lockheed Martin Electronics and Missiles Division during a competition to build the new missile. Lockheed Martin eventually won the competition, and is expected to produce over 3,000 of the stealthy missiles. It is a tight fit, but JASSM does fit on the F-117A. *Lockheed Martin Skunk Works*

Out of the Black—Senior Trend Becomes the F-117A

There has been a lot of speculation about how and when the F-117A designation was applied to the SENIOR TREND program. As a designation it makes little sense given what has been publicly acknowledged by the Air Force, especially since there apparently was no F-112 through F-116. There is no real point speculating over where the designation came from, but sometime in the mid-1980s as SENIOR TREND began to emerge from its black world, the aircraft became known as F-117As.

The aircraft's initial operational shortcomings convinced the Air Force to fund upgrades to improve the aircraft. The modifications were aimed at improving the aircraft's weapons carrying capabilities, and the Offensive Capability Improvement Program (OCIP) consisted of three distinct phases. The $191-million OCIP I was also known as the Weapons Systems Computational Subsystem (WSCS) upgrade, and replaced the aircraft's original three Delco M362F mission computers with three Mil-Std-1750A-compliant IBM AP-102 computers communicating over dual-redundant Mil-Std-1553B data busses (computer networks). The adaptation of a Mil-Std-1750A-compliant computer (and its associated data busses) allowed for the integration of standard Air Force "smart" weapons without a lengthy development cycle.

The first offensive weapon to take advantage of this on the F-117A was the GBU-27 Paveway III laser-guided bomb. The Paveway III system was a tremendous improvement over the earlier laser-guided bombs, but unfortunately it proved to be much more difficult to add to the F-117A than had been anticipated. The original Paveway III was the GBU-24, and much like the SENIOR TREND, it had been developed in considerable secrecy. As a result, the F-117A's weapons bays were too small to accommodate weapons; the tail fins were too large and the guidance section adapter was too long. The ever resourceful Air Force and Skunk Works personnel used the Paveway III guidance section attached to a Mk 84

2,000-pound bomb equipped with the older (and smaller) Paveway II tail unit. Although this decreased some of the improved accuracy of the Paveway III, the new bomb was small enough to fit inside the F-117A weapons bays. A production version was subsequently ordered under the GBU-27 designation.

OCIP I also added new composite weapons bay doors that allowed both weapons bays to be opened simultaneously. The first F-117A equipped with the OCIP I modifications was re-delivered to the air force in November 1987, and all F-117As had been modified by June 1992. The second phase of OCIP addressed some concerns pilots had expressed about the cockpit equipment. The F-117A had originally used monochrome displays for most flight instrumentation and FLIR imagery. These displays were replaced with new, color multifunction displays, taken from late-model F/A-18s, along with a new digital moving map display. OCIP II conversions began in 1988, and all aircraft had been modified by the end of 1993.

OCIP III was aimed at replacing some avionics that had become obsolete and were no longer supported in the maintenance channels. The original inertial guidance system (INS) was replaced with a ring-laser gyro, and greatly reduced the pre-mission setup. During Desert Storm the usefulness of the Global Positioning System (GPS) became fully understood, and like many Air Force aircraft, a GPS receiver was subsequently installed on the F-117A using a stealthy GPS antenna developed as part of the ATF (F-22) program.

The exotic RAM has even received some upgrades, mainly thanks to newer products developed for other programs such as the B-2 and F-22. The original RAM added almost 2,000 pounds to the empty weight of the aircraft. The new RAM, in addition to being slightly more effective, has reduced this to approximately 400 pounds. Lockheed subsequently developed a spray-on RAM that is easier to maintain and somewhat more effective. There was a great deal

There are exceptions to F-117As not having unique markings. This aircraft was painted in late 1983 to mark the turnover of command of the F-117 test detachment from Lt. Col. Roger Moseley to Paul Tackamore at 14:00 hours on December 14, 1983. *Tony Landis Collection*

of difficulty getting the spray-on RAM to obtain a uniform thickness, but improved processes and materials have overcome these problems.

Originally the F-117A went into combat and observed complete radio silence to ensure the enemy could not locate the aircraft by tracking its emissions. In late 1998, flight testing began on the "Integrated Real-time Information into the Cockpit/Real-time Information Out of the Cockpit for Combat Aircraft (IRRCA)" system for the F-117A. This is a secure high-bandwidth data link between either a high-flying U-2 or a satellite and the F-117A. The system uses an upward pointed low-probability-of-intercept (LPI) antenna and burst transmission, frequency-hopping techniques that are virtually impossible to trace from the ground, although it is possible an AWACS-type aircraft might detect them momentarily. Incoming data from the link is displayed on the color moving map display and can include status reports, updated target imagery, and new navigational or targeting data.

The total costs for the F-117 program have been released as just over $6.5 billion. Each aircraft cost $42.6 million for a total of $2.5 billion for procurement. Development added $2 billion, and military construction amounted to $295 million. The cost of various upgrades accounts for the difference.

The YF-22

In many ways the YF-22 effort took Lockheed back to the concept first used on the XP-80 prototype effort. Skunk Works will design and assemble two prototype aircraft, but future production aircraft would be built by another Lockheed organization; in this case, in Marietta, Georgia. The great secrecy surrounding stealth technology dictated a very quiet program, much like the original XP-80. A government decision midway through the design competition to limit the fly-off to only two manufacturers would bring a situation that Skunk Works was very unfamiliar with—collaborating with other large companies to produce a "composite" design made up of parts from each manufacturer. This situation would certainly take longer than a typical Skunk Works project.

In November 1981 the Air Force initiated the Advanced Tactical Fighter (ATF) program, also called SENIOR SKY, to replace the McDonnell Douglas F-15 Eagle. Nine airframe manufacturers—Boeing, Fairchild-Republic, General Dynamics, Grumman, Lockheed, LTV, McDonnell Douglas, Northrop, and Rockwell International—were asked to participate in preliminary concept studies. These studies identified several specific performance characteristics that were desirable, including the ability to "supercruise" at supersonic speeds without an afterburner. Contrary to popular belief, the ATF would not be the first military aircraft capable of supercruising; this distinction belongs to the General Dynamics B-58 Hustler. The B-58, however, had to employ its afterburners or dive steeply to accelerate through the transonic drag to get to the flight condition where it could supercruise. The F-16XL and newer-model F-15s and F-16s are also capable of supersonic flight without an afterburner, but again usually need their afterburners for the initial push through the sound barrier.

The companies in the studies submitted a wide range of configurations in response to the SENIOR SKY studies. Skunk Works submitted a single-seat derivative of the YF-12A optimized for air-to-ground missions that carried several kinetic-energy penetrator weapons in a central weapons bay where the radar officer used to sit. In May 1983, after evaluating the results of the SENIOR SKY studies, the Air Force issued a request for proposals for ATF concept definition studies. Boeing, General Dynamics, Grumman, McDonnell Douglas, Northrop, Rockwell, and Skunk Works began to prepare proposals for submittal in mid-June. However, just before the deadline, the Air Force requested that each contractor include a discussion of their stealth-related skills and experience. The original proposals were limited to 30 pages, and the stealth addendum—to be submitted as a separate, highly classified volume—had to fit on five pages.

"Originally, the ATF program did not contain stealth," explains Al Piccirillo, the director of the Air Force ATF System Program Office at the time. "People on the program were aware of what was going on in the F-117 and the B-2 programs. We would have been really stupid to develop an advanced fighter without using this new technology. Without stealth, I am not sure the air force could have justified ATF."

In their response, Skunk Works made a radical departure from its original design and started from scratch with an F-117 derivative in its proposal for the concept definition phase. "Clearly, ATF was going to be superstealth and not a cousin of YF-12 or SR-71," said Bart Osborne, program manager for Lockheed's Tactical Aircraft Systems. All effort on the YF-12 derivative was shelved, and a faceted design based on the F-117 took its

The first YF-22 demonstrator carried civil registration N22YF. The aircraft had been built by Skunk Works, and was rolled out in a ceremony at Palmdale on August 29, 1990. The YF-22 made its first flight on September 29, 1990, with Lockheed test pilot Dave Furguson at the controls. The flight left Palmdale and arrived at nearby Edwards AFB. *Lockheed Martin Skunk Works*

place. The primary differences were the use of a high-mounted wing, a more conventional empennage (horizontal and vertical stabilizers), and inlets placed below and behind the leading edge of the wing. Lockheed surprisingly still did not have the ability to analyze a curved stealthy shape, and had become convinced that if they could not analyze a design as a stealthy shape, then it could not be stealthy. Skunk Works' submittal for the concept definition phase was not received well by the Air Force; it placed last in the field of seven.

Nevertheless, each of the seven companies that bid, including Lockheed, received a $1-million contract for

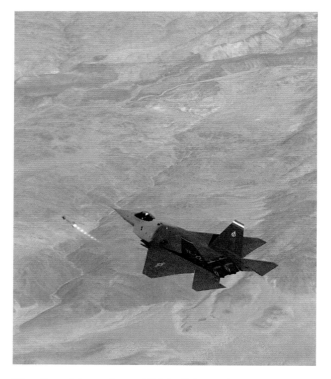

The first firing of an AIM-9 Sidewinder occurred on November 28, 1990, with the first firing of an AIM-120 AMRAAM on December 20. This is the second prototype (N22YX). The first aircraft had a red stripe on the top of the vertical stabilizer, while the second aircraft had a blue stripe. *Lockheed Martin Skunk Works*

continued studies through May 1985 when the air force received final briefings from each contractor. After evaluating the results in September 1985, the Air Force issued requests for proposals for the demonstration/validation phase where four winning companies would be given about $100 million each to demonstrate the technologies needed to build their design. The deadline for the proposals was set for that December.

After a poor showing in the concept definition phase, Lockheed had to turn around its ATF program before the next proposal was due. Skunk Works had not faired well in recent design competitions. The company had proposed a faceted design for the Advanced Technology Bomber that became the B-2 and lost. Skunk Works had also used a faceted design in the Navy's Advanced Tactical Aircraft (A-12) competition and lost. The Air Force's response to Lockheed's concept exploration proposal forced the company to rethink its commitment to faceting for stealth.

"We simply started drawing curved shapes," recalls Osborne, "even though we could not run the designs through our analytical software models. When we went to curved airplanes, we began to get more acceptable supersonic and maneuver performance. Instead of relying on software models, we built curved shapes and tested them on the company's radar range. The curved shapes performed quite well in the radar tests."

The Skunk Works configuration quickly progressed from faceted to smooth. The proposed design had a streamlined nose and trapezoidal wing platform with a positive sweep on both the leading and trailing edges. Two large vertical stabilizers were canted outwards. The leading and trailing edge sweep angles of all of the surfaces were aligned at common angles, and the design had a wide strake that ran in a straight line from the wing leading edge outboard of the inlets to the point of the nose.

Lockheed built a large-scale model of this curved configuration to test on the company's radar range. The data from these tests went into the company's proposal for the dem/val phase. According to Osborne: "The real question the Air Force had was whether Lockheed could design a curved stealthy airplane. . . . We showed them with the range model that we could do curves."

As with the previous phase, the Air Force delayed the submittal date for the dem/val proposals. This time the deadline was put off for prototyping. Instead of approximately $100-million contracts for four winners,

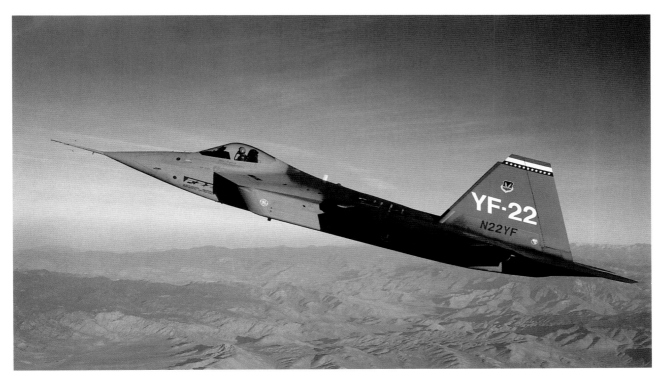

There is little external evidence of the Skunk Works involvement with the YF-22, but a close examination will show a small white skunk logo just behind the registration number on the vertical stabilizer. The first aircraft used General Electric YF120-GE-100 engines and carried a small white GE logo on the air intake. The second aircraft carried a full-color Pratt & Whitney logo in the same location. *Lockheed Martin Skunk Works*

the Air Force added flying prototypes to the program and would award only two contracts of about $700 million each. The competitors were given 60 extra days to describe how they would design, build, and test two flying prototypes. The amendment also had a cover letter that encouraged the companies to team up. According to Piccirillo: "The Air Force encouraged teaming because it wanted the best resources from industry to be brought to bear on the program. The program was going to be expensive and big. The

more commitment we had from industry, the more likely the program was to succeed."

Almost immediately, a complicated dance began among the contractors to see who wanted to partner with whom. Representatives from Boeing, General Dynamics, and Lockheed signed a teaming agreement in June 1986. Northrop and McDonnell Douglas announced their team two months later. The two remaining companies, Grumman and Rockwell, did not partner up.

The second EMD F-22 made its first flight on June 29, 1998, from Dobbins AFB in Marietta, Georgia. The aircraft weapons bays are integrated into the side of the fuselage immediately behind the intake, and the main landing gear wells are located behind the weapons bays. All EMD and production Raptors will use Pratt & Whitney thrust-vectoring engines. *Lockheed Martin Skunk Works*

Collaboration did not stop each company from submitting their own designs. There was not enough time to create a composite design, so the proposals were submitted by each company as they had been written. The teaming agreement among Boeing, General Dynamics, and Lockheed called for the winning company to be the team lead. The teaming deal was "blind" and none of the participants were allowed to see the other contenders' aircraft or program plans before the contract was awarded.

The announcement came on October 31, 1986, and named Lockheed and Northrop as the winners of the two $691-million contracts to build the YF-22 and YF-23, respectively. On the following Monday morning, representatives from Boeing, General Dynamics, and Lockheed met for the first time as a team at the Skunk Works facility in Burbank. About 100 engineers and managers crowded into a large high-security conference room in Building 360 where representatives from each company were allotted two hours to present their proposed ATF concept. The all-day show-and-tell was unprecedented for everyone in attendance. Never before had they shared everything they knew about a program with an audience considered to be the competition only a week before.

"That Monday was the most fascinating day I ever spent in the aircraft business," remembers Randy Kent, the ATF program director for General Dynamics from 1985 to 1991. "Typically, we never know what other teams have done for months, if ever, after a contract is awarded. For ATF, however, each company made the same presentation at Burbank it made to the air force. We all put our models, layouts, and drawings on the table. Everyone received detailed views of what everyone else had done to that point in the program. The experience was amazing."

Another equally astonishing meeting happened the next day. The air force briefed the three companies on how their proposals had been evaluated. The actual evaluation charts used when selecting the two winners were shown, and about 70 strengths and 30 weaknesses for each proposal were discussed. "This was the only time in my career that I saw an official government evaluation of what we and two of our strongest competitors had submitted for a competition," remembers Sherm Mullin, the program director for Skunk Works.

The ATF effort resulted in one of the first fighters to be designed from the beginning with computers, and computer-aided design proved critical to completing the configuration studies that would lead to the YF-22 prototype. The first electronic drawings were formally released on April 1, 1988, and led to the rough-cutting of a mid-fuselage titanium bulkhead in Fort Worth on April 27. The mid-fuselage was built in a secure area at the north end of the F-16 final assembly line. Production of the forward fuselage began

soon after with the nose wheel forward bulkhead at the Skunk Works facilities in Burbank. The aft fuselage and wings took shape during the same time at the Boeing facilities in Seattle. It took two years to fabricate the two YF-22 prototypes.

The YF-22 was unveiled to the public on August 29, 1990, and the prototype made its maiden flight on September 29 when Lockheed test pilot Dave Furguson flew it from Palmdale to Edwards AFB. The second prototype flew for the first time on October 30. The flight rate ramped up from 13 in October, to 22 in November, and 38 in December. The two prototypes accumulated over 90 flight hours in 74 flights, reached speeds over Mach 2, maneuvered at 7 g, and flew at a 60-degree angle of attack. Also included was a demonstration of its super-cruising ability.

In the meantime, the Lockheed and Northrop teams wrote their final production proposals. On April 23, 1991, Secretary of the Air Force Donald Rice announced the winner of the ATF program and noted that the Lockheed and Pratt & Whitney design "clearly offered better capability at lower cost, thereby providing the Air Force with a true best value." The original full-scale development contract called for nine single-seat and two two-seat aircraft, along with two ground-test airframes. The subsequent production phase originally included the production of 750 fighters with first delivery scheduled for 2005. Late in the dem/val phase, the total was reduced to 648 aircraft, and subsequent post–Cold War funding and threat analyses have now reduced the number to 339 aircraft.

After Lockheed was announced as the winner, Skunk Works largely backed out of the F-22 program and left it, as tradition dictated, to the mainstream Lockheed organizations in Marietta and Fort Worth. This does not mean that Skunk Works is totally uninvolved. They will still provide engineering and technical support as needed, but another fighter project had already begun at Skunk Works.

Four

The second DarkStar at the Lockheed RCS measurement range near Helendale, California. After the crash of the first air vehicle, this DarkStar would be modified with the improvements identified after the accident investigation and used for the remainder of the flight test program. The large pole the aircraft is mounted on can be retracted into a work area underground to keep it out of sight of prying eyes and satellites. *Lockheed Martin Skunk Works photo by Al Ross*

More Stealth—
THE JSF AND DARKSTAR

Joint Strike Fighter

During 1986, the Defense Advanced Research Projects Agency (DARPA) began collaborating with the United Kingdom on an Advanced Short Takeoff and Vertical Landing (ASTOVL) aircraft to replace the Harrier in British service, and to possibly replace the F-16 for the U.S. Air Force. Between 1989 and 1991, DARPA funded aircraft design studies by General Dynamics, McDonnell Douglas, and Skunk Works, as well as propulsion studies by General Electric and Pratt & Whitney.

The studies were to concentrate on two primary areas of vertical flight. The first area was to find how to eliminate the hot high-velocity exhaust gases generated by direct-lift systems such as the Harrier. These gases pose serious threats to people and material in the immediate vicinity of an aircraft during landing operations. Consider the following excerpt from the AV-8B flight manual:

"Energy Levels in V/STOL Flight: The energy output from the four nozzles in V/STOL flight is about 30,000 horsepower. The reaction controls at full control demand have an energy output of several thousand horsepower. The front nozzles exhaust emerges at about 700 knots, 105 degrees Celsius (220 degrees Fahrenheit), and 16 psi. The rear nozzles exhaust emerges at about 1,050 knots, 645 degrees Celsius (1,195 degrees Fahrenheit), and 11 psi. The reaction control valves exhaust emerges at about 1,500 knots, 400 degrees Celsius (750 degrees Fahenheit) and 150 psi. Although velocity, pressure, and temperature drop off with distance, the exhaust velocity at ground level in a low hover can be 300–400 knots at 4 psi. If this pressure is permitted to build up under a surface such as a landing mat or manhole cover, the lifting force becomes tremendous. A pressure of 4 psi will lift 4-foot-thick

The Boeing/BAE Systems Harrier is one of the aircraft that is supposed to be replaced by the Joint Strike Fighter. The Harrier has suffered from some unique operational concerns, including extremely hot exhaust under the aircraft during vertical flight/hover. Regardless, the Harrier has proven to be a remarkably versatile attack aircraft that will be a hard act to follow. The Harrier achieves vertical flight by rotating four nozzles—two at the rear vector hot turbine exhaust, and two at the front vector cooler compressor air. *Lockheed Martin Skunk Works*

concrete or 8-inch-thick steel. The Harrier has proven to be an efficient manhole cover remover, although it displays no discretion on depositing them after removal. The aircraft has raised an 11-ton mat 4 feet above the ground. Pneumatically supported mats do not soften the landing; therefore, all landing mats should be thoroughly sealed including the perimeter. The aircraft should never cross the edge of a mat in V/STOL flight at less than 50 feet."

The second problem DARPA wished to address was stealth. The available knowledge on stealth characteristics seemed to indicate that a single rear-mounted engine exhaust nozzle was the best way to maintain low-observable (LO) characteristics. The use of four rotating nozzles, such as the nozzles on the Harrier, destroyed any other stealth aspects of an aircraft design. A way would have to be found to divert some of the engine's energy forward while at the same time keeping the jet velocity and hot gas ejection much lower than on Harrier while using a single nozzle.

During early 1990, two engineers at Skunk Works, Paul M. Bevilaqua and Paul K. Shumpert, devised a method to meet these requirements and were awarded a patent in 1993. In essence, a normal turbofan engine is located in the conventional location in the aft fuselage and fitted with an exhaust nozzle that can be rotated 90 degrees downward to provide vertical lift at the rear of the aircraft. A separate fan, driven by a shaft from the front of the engine, is located in the forward part of the aircraft and pointed downward. This provides lift for the front of the aircraft. The fact that the forward fan is mechanically powered from the main engine means that its exhaust is relatively cool. When the aircraft is in normal "up-and-away" flight, the forward fan is de-coupled from the engine by means of a clutch, and the intake and exhaust doors are closed to present a smooth appearance that maintains the stealth characteristics of the aircraft. This breakthrough gave DARPA hope that a workable design could be developed.

DARPA devised a plan for the development of a short takeoff/vertical landing (STOVL) aircraft that involved multiple contractors for about a year of design studies, and then two contractors would be selected to conduct a three-year Critical Technologies Validation (CTV) program beginning in March 1993. The CTV would involve building large-scale (80 percent of full size) models and testing them in a variety of facilities such as the hover laboratory at NASA Ames. This would be followed in mid-1996 by the selection of a single contractor to design and build two full-scale prototypes. The program would then be turned over to the Navy for the development of production models. Before this plan could be carried out, DARPA discovered that its preliminary lift-fan design could easily be converted into a conventional fighter by eliminating the lift-fan and using the space in the airframe for additional fuel or avionics. This allowed a single basic aircraft design to meet the STOVL needs of the Marine Corps, and the conventional strike aircraft requirements of the Air Force and Navy. One of DARPA's goals was to reduce the cost of weapons systems, and a

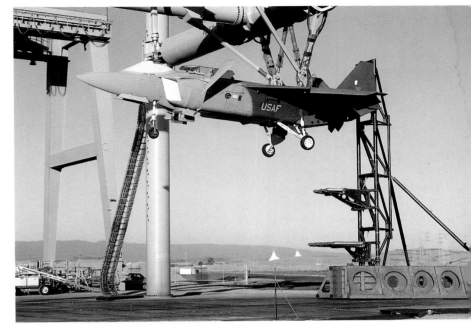

Above: The Lockheed CALF model was tested in both the Outdoor Aerodynamic Research Facility (OARF) and the 80-by-120-foot wind tunnel at the NASA Ames Research Center. The model featured a working propulsion system based around a Pratt & Whitney F-100 turbofan engine, and had many features that were generally similar to the YF-22. The CALF model said "USAF" on one side and "MARINES" on the other. *Lockheed Martin Skunk Works*

Left: This is an artist's concept variously described as an ASTOVL design or an early JAST concept. This design used large intakes along the sides of the fuselage, small canards, and a large main wing. Canard solutions appeared attractive because they put the mass of the wing well aft. This was helpful for vertical landings since it reduced the need to shift the center of thrust forward. A pair of weapons bays on the underside of the air intakes could each accommodate a single 2,000-pound laser-guided bomb. *Lockheed Martin Skunk Works*

The Lockheed JSF shares an obvious family heritage with the F-22. In the STOVL variant, a shaft-driven lift-fan is located directly behind the cockpit. The main landing gear retracts forward and inward into the wing-fuselage fairing. This allows a heavier landing gear to be installed on the carrier variant by using a slightly larger fairing, an elegant design that maximizes the commonality of primary structure between the variants. *Lockheed Martin Skunk Works drawing by K. Price Randel*

revival of the commonality concept that had played so poorly during the McNamara regime appeared to offer a chance of success this time around.

The name of the program was changed from ASTOVL to CALF—Common Affordable Lightweight Fighter. Four companies—Boeing, McDonnell Douglas, Northrop, and Skunk Works—were invited to bid on a program to build two demonstrator aircraft; one STOVL and one conventional. The CALF contracts were awarded to McDonnell Douglas and Skunk Works in March 1993, and both companies proposed stealthy designs using rear-mounted main wings and canards equipped with the requisite internal weapons bays. A single turbofan engine was mounted in the rear fuselage, and both designs had a lift-fan located directly behind the cockpit, but the manner in which they were driven was different. In keeping with the original patent concept,

The first X-35 comes together at Palmdale in early 1999. The bay for the lift-fan is directly behind the cockpit. The cockpit itself is very spacious, and designed to fit all potential pilots from a variety of countries. This is a great consideration given the export sales potential of the JSF. To reduce the time necessary to build the prototypes, Skunk Works used fairly conventional assembly techniques. Concurrently, a parallel program, the Aircraft Affordability Demonstration, was undertaken to demonstrate the low-cost concepts envisioned for production aircraft. *Lockheed Martin Skunk Works photo by Marty Wolin*

Lockheed used a clutch at the front of the engine to divert rotational power to an Allison-developed lift-fan. McDonnell Douglas decided to forego the direct mechanical connection and divert some of the high-pressure bleed air from the fan section of the main engine and use it to spin the lift-fan's turbine. In both concepts, the total airflow almost doubled in the vertical lift mode and boosted low-speed thrust while the jet velocity was reduced considerably.

Both contractors designed aircraft that could be built in two versions—one with the lift-fan and one without. Since only one company would be selected to build actual prototypes, DARPA assigned a single designation to the program: the X-32A without the lift-fan, and the X-32B with a lift-fan. As with the original ASTOVL program, the United Kingdom was always intended as an equal partner in CALF, but the security restrictions surrounding stealth technology held up a formal agreement until early 1994.

During 1993 the Department of Defense conducted a Bottom-Up Review (BUR) that determined it was not economical to develop both the air force's Multi-Role Fighter (MRF) and the navy's Advanced Strike Fighter (A/F-X), and both programs were subsequently canceled. Nevertheless, the BUR concurred that an advanced strike aircraft was going to be required by all three fixed-wing air arms, and recommended the initiation of a Joint Advanced Strike Technology (JAST) program to develop the technology that would be necessary for the next-generation strike weapons system. The intent of the program was to demonstrate various technologies that would substantially lower the cost and improve the effectiveness of any future aircraft. JAST in itself was not intended to be an operational fighter.

The question was, where did this leave the CALF project? It could be argued that CALF and JAST were complementary. JAST would focus on operational technologies such as sensors and weapons, while CALF would demonstrate propulsion and airframe technologies. It

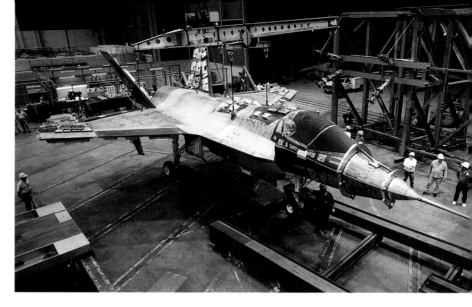

The first X-35 prototype at Palmdale is structurally complete and is almost ready to move into the paint shop. The large canopy has excellent forward and side visibility to help pilots during strike missions, but is somewhat lacking in rearward visibility. Both prototypes are fitted with air data booms from the nose to use during the test program; the production aircraft will not have these. *Lockheed Martin Skunk Works*

could also be argued that with no clear-cut goal in mind, JAST would become just another sinkhole for money with nothing to show in the end. Nobody counted on the leadership provided by the first JAST program manager. Air Force Maj. Gen. George K. Muellner, an experienced combat pilot himself, had decided that JAST needed to produce an aircraft that could reasonably replace the A-10, F-16, Harrier, early F/A-18s, and possibly the Jaguars, Tornados, and other light strike aircraft in service around the world. The result would be a universal fighter that could be built by the thousands at a reasonable price.

To assist in achieving these goals, JAST turned to modern management techniques (integrated product teams, etc.) and large-scale simulations that allowed

Both X-35 vehicles are shown here as they near completion in Palmdale. The semi-chine along the forward fuselage is very reminiscent of the F-22, but the air intake has taken on a design of its own. This is largely due to the complex supersonic inlet used on the F-22, which is not needed on the JSF since it is not meant to fly at Mach 2. This allowed designers to concentrate on reducing the radar signature of the opening without being as concerned about airflow. *Lockheed Martin Skunk Works*

quick, accurate, documented trade studies. The two major problems to be overcome were the reluctance of anybody to embrace the commonality concept again after the almost complete failure of the F-111 program 30 years earlier, and the navy's preference for two-engine aircraft.

The first hurdle was overcome by the simulations, and the fact that modern technology had eliminated many of the points that had hampered the development of the F-111. Avionics had become frequently common between aircraft already, as had engines; and computer-controlled manufacturing techniques seemed to allow airframes to be tailored easily on the production line. The second hurdle was largely overcome through analysis. With the assistance of the Georgia Tech Research Institute and Johns Hopkins University, the JAST program office successfully demonstrated that a single-engine aircraft had equal survivability compared to a two-engine fighter under most circumstances. The Navy was not totally convinced, but realized there was little point in arguing it since limited funds would not allow a second development effort.

Muellner also saw the CALF program as an essential piece in developing any future fighter program, and began to actively include it in plans for JAST. As JAST began to head toward a production program, interest in it increased significantly. The stakes were enormous. If a production JAST was adopted by all three U.S. military air arms, the total production run could top 3,000 aircraft. Add British and other foreign sales, and the production effort could rival that of the F-104 and F-16, and add up to 6,000 aircraft. By late 1994, four companies were actively preparing to compete for JAST contracts—Boeing, Lockheed, McDonnell Douglas, and Northrop Grumman. The government subsequently announced that it would select two contractors to each build two flyable demonstrators.

In late 1994, Northrop Grumman teamed with McDonnell Douglas and British Aerospace (BAe, now BAE Systems). This team appeared to be the one to beat. It combined all of the West's experienced VTOL contractors (McDonnell Douglas and BAe built the Harrier), the navy's premier carrier fighter manufacturers (McDonnell Douglas built the Hornet; Grumman had built almost every other navy fighter for 50 years), and the nation's most modern stealth manufacturer (Northrop built the B-2 Spirit bomber). If experience counted, this team had it. This left Boeing and Lockheed, who discussed teaming, but each was too stubborn to give up their own design in favor of the other's. Lockheed had extensive stealth experience with the HAVE

BLUE and F-117 programs, but had not built a true operational fighter since the F-104, or to some people, the P-80. Boeing was in even worse shape. They had never built a manned supersonic aircraft, had not built a fighter of any description in almost 50 years, and had no known experience with stealth technology.

Lockheed assigned the JAST program to Skunk Works, where the CALF program was already in full swing. The same basic design proposed for CALF (rear wing and forward canard) was used in the early JAST studies. In 1995 after Lockheed acquired the former Convair operations that had belonged to General Dynamics, the JAST program was relocated from Skunk Works to Fort Worth, and things began to change. All through the CALF and early JAST program, Skunk Works had proposed a design with a forward canard. This had begun to create troubles when the navy's requirements were taken into account. Landing on a carrier requires a relatively slow approach speed at a flat attitude, implying a large wing area and effective flap control. To achieve these requirements, the canard was beginning to grow unacceptably large. When the design got to Fort Worth, it was immediately faced with F-16 designer Harry Hillaker's motto, "the optimum location for a canard is on somebody else's airplane." The canard was history. Given the long tradition in Fort Worth, a delta-wing configuration was examined in detail, but in the end a conventional tailed design similar to the F-22 was chosen. This was undoubtedly much to the relief of the Navy. The service had a very limited, but unhappy experience with rear-wing carrier aircraft (Vought F7U and Douglas F4D).

A request for proposals by the government was released in March 1996 with a submittal deadline in early June. At the same time, the name of the program was changed to Joint Strike Fighter (JSF), and reflected the new-found production aspirations instead of being strictly a technology demonstration. On November 16, 1996, Secretary of Defense William Perry announced that Boeing and Lockheed Martin had been selected to build the JSF prototypes. The McDonnell

Engine run-up tests at Palmdale show how the shock cones exit the single Pratt & Whitney JSF119 turbofan. Many outside observers are worried about the reliability of the F119 in the JSF application, although testing so far has shown the unit to be outstanding. What is more worrisome at the moment is the shaft-driven lift-fan which has suffered a variety of minor glitches that have hampered testing. Lockheed Martin expresses complete confidence in the design, and points out that all technical advances suffer early teething problems. *Lockheed Martin Skunk Works*

Douglas team was shocked, and Boeing was exuberant. It did not matter, because several weeks later Boeing announced it was purchasing McDonnell Douglas.

The Competition

It is easy to dismiss the Joint Strike Fighter as just another fighter. It's not a terribly sexy one at that, but the scope of the program is enormous. It is very likely that 3,000 to 6,000 JSFs will be manufactured over the life of a program that has a potential value of over $400 billion. The stakes are tremendous, and both Boeing and

The word out of most people's mouth when they first see the Boeing X-32 JSF demonstrator is "ugly." However, the X-32 is no longer truly representative of the expected production machine. The design evolved considerably while the prototype was being built. The Boeing design made its maiden flight on September 18, 2000, from Palmdale to Edwards AFB. Skunk Works followed on October 24, 2000. Each company has stated that an analysis of past competitions shows no clear correlation between which design flew first and the ultimate winner. *Boeing*

Lockheed Martin are investing a lot of resources to ensure they win.

The JSF program is intended to produce three different aircraft that maintain maximum possible commonality: A conventional takeoff version is destined for the Air Force; a conventional takeoff version with a larger wing is meant for Navy service aboard aircraft carriers; and a STOVL version is being designed for the Marine Corps, Royal Navy, and Royal Air Force. The largest potential export market is for the air force version, although countries that have operated the Harrier (Spain, Italy, India, and Thailand) may well opt for the STOVL version.

The initial contracts awarded to Boeing and Lockheed Martin are for two Concept Demonstration Aircraft (CDA) powered by modified F119 engines since it is the only current production engine of the correct thrust rating. These demonstrators have three primary purposes: to prove the basic flying qualities of the design, to demonstrate the low-speed (landing) performance required for carrier operations, and to prove that

the selected STOVL concept works. The last one will likely be the hardest to achieve. The CDAs are not considered true prototypes of production fighters and are designated in the X-series instead of the YF-series. The Boeing design will reuse the X-32 designation originally assigned to the CALF program, and Lockheed Martin was assigned X-35 for their aircraft.

While most of the attention is focused on the demonstrator aircraft, a major part of the competition is the design of the Preferred Weapon System Concept (PWSC). This is what will become the production aircraft that will fly as part of the engineering and manufacturing development (EMD) phase. Also on the sidelines but extremely important to the overall program are a variety of technology maturation programs. Some of these programs predate the JAST program, such as the Joint Integrated Subsystems Technology (J/IST) project that is working on electric control surface actuators and other advanced subsystems. Other programs, including most of the avionics development, were initiated during the early days of JAST.

The military expects "dumb" (unguided) bombs to be obsolete by the time the JSF enters service, so Boeing and Lockheed are designing their aircraft around the latest smart bombs. The requirements are that all versions must carry two AIM-120 AMRAAM air-to-air missiles, and two Joint Direct Attack Munitions (JDAM) in internal weapons bays. The Navy and Air Force have specified the 2,000-pound GBU-31 JDAM, while the marines are content with the 1,000-pound GBU-32 version. The Air Force variant will carry an internal cannon (probably the 27-mm cannon built by Boeing based upon the Mauser-Werke BK27 design), but the Navy and Marine variants will carry their gun in a removable pack that can be installed in one of the weapons bays. Unlike most recent stealth aircraft, the JSF will also be equipped to carry weapons externally. The idea is that for the first few days of an air campaign, JSF will attack using weapons carried internally in order to maintain stealth. After defenses are somewhat beaten down and stealth is less important, additional weapons will be carried on four hard-points under the wings to allow more targets to be engaged per sortie. Range requirements differ and the Marines and Air Force specify a 450-nautical mile-unrefueled range, while the navy needs 550-nautical mile range.

Although Boeing acquired McDonnell Douglas in 1996, they did not come away with the companies that had originally teamed with the St. Louis firm. Within six months of the CDA announcement, both Northrop Grumman and BAE Systems had joined the Lockheed team. The project is being managed in Fort Worth (what was Lockheed Martin Tactical Aircraft Systems is now the Fort Worth Operations of Lockheed Martin Aeronautical Systems [LMTAS]), but the two X-35 demonstrators are being built by Skunk Works in Palmdale.

The X-35 is clearly related to the F-22, and shares similar aerodynamics and approaches to stealth. The main difference between the JSF and its fighter cousin, apart from size, is the propulsion system. The X-35 has a single engine instead of two and uses a new diverterless

inlet with a bump on the inner wall instead of the traditional splitter plate, much like the half-cone devices used on the original F-104. The X-35 also dispenses with thrust vectoring on its engine nozzle, although it can swivel 90 degrees downward on the STOVL variant. The three-bearing nozzle design was patterned loosely after the one used on the Russian Yak-141.

The X-35B STOVL aircraft is identical to the conventional design except for a slight bulge in the spine to cover the lift-fan, and a shorter canopy. The lift-fan supports almost half the weight of the aircraft during hover, and produces 18,000 pounds-thrust. Bleed air from the engine fan (not the lift-fan) feeds two roll control thrusters at the wing fold line and provides control at speeds when the aerodynamic surfaces are not effective. The STOVL version also has an auxiliary inlet for the main engine on top of the fuselage to eliminate FOD concerns during hover.

Getting Ready

The Lockheed X-35A JSF demonstrator made its first flight on October 24, 2000. Lockheed Martin test pilot Tom Morgenfeld lifted the aircraft off of Palmdale's main runway at 9:06 A.M. and landed the aircraft at nearby Edwards AFB. A speed of 250 knots and an altitude of 10,000 feet were attained during the flight. By November 6 the aircraft was ready for its fifth flight, which was flown by Air Force pilot Lt. Col. Paul Smith. Smith's 36-minute flight reached 360 knots at 10,000 feet. He proclaimed the demonstrator an "excellent handling aircraft, very thrust-responsive; it flies like a world-class fighter." The next day the JSF conducted its first aerial refueling from a KC-135, again with Smith at the controls.

On November 21 the first JSF demonstrator exceeded the speed of sound for the first time, attaining Mach 1.05 at 25,000 feet. Test pilot Tom Morgenfeld was the pilot and the flight was the 25th of the program. Earlier in the day during the 24th flight, Morgenfeld had made six field carrier landing practice demonstrations,

In addition to a larger wing, the Navy version of the JSF is expected to use stronger landing gear with a dual nose wheel arrangement. The faceted landing gear doors shown here are features not present on the X-35 demonstrators. The Navy version of the Lockheed JSF will also use a different canopy to provide slightly improved vision for carrier landings. *Lockheed Martin Skunk Works drawing by P. Benson*

and previewed the aircraft's low-speed carrier approach handling qualities in advance of upcoming tests of the second demonstrator.

With its flight testing complete, the X-35A returned to Lockheed Martin's Palmdale facility to be fitted with a shaft-driven lift-fan propulsion system. It will be renamed the X-35B and will begin ground testing in preparation for its STOVL demonstrations scheduled to begin during the spring of 2001. The lift-fan was installed on January 11, 2001, and the aircraft began testing in a "hover pit" during February.

At 9:23 A.M on December 16, 2000, Lockheed Martin test pilot Joe Sweeney took-off in the X-35C carrier variant (CV) from the Lockheed Martin Aeronautics plant in Palmdale and flew for 27 minutes before touching down at Edwards. The aircraft climbed to 10,000 feet and accelerated to 250 knots. Sweeney, a former Navy attack pilot, cycled the landing gear and performed aircraft flying-qualities evaluations, including rolls, sideslips, and overall systems checks. LCDR Brian Goszkowicz became the first navy pilot to fly the X-35C on December 22, 2000. During the 42-minute flight, Goszkowicz reached an altitude of 10,000 feet and a speed of 250 knots, and described the X-35C's flight path as "smooth and predictable."

The X-35C flew to Patuxent River Naval Air Station on February 10, 2001, completing the first transcontinental flight of JSF demonstrator. While at Pax River the aircraft will conduct a series of carrier suitability demonstrations using the mock carrier deck painted on the Pax runway. Tom Burbage, executive vice president and general manager of the Lockheed Martin JSF program, and former Navy carrier pilot, said: "We are happy to be back at Patuxent River, testing carrier aircraft with the Navy. We strongly believe that sea-level testing is necessary to give us a true picture of the X-35C's carrier suitability."

Although Skunk Works was the lead organization in the original JAST program, when the work was transferred to Fort Worth, it largely left Skunk Works as a major subcontractor responsible primarily for building the two X-35 demonstrators. Skunk Works engineers have remained involved in the design effort for the PWSC aircraft, but they are far outnumbered by their Fort Worth counterparts. Skunk Works test pilots will undoubtedly participate in the flight tests, but again they will be outnumbered by pilots from Texas.

Even before the Skunk Works demonstrators had begun test flying, problems were being discovered. For instance, an overheating bearing slightly delayed testing of the STOVL propulsion system. The problem involved a bearing at the front of the F119 engine where power is transferred to the clutch and gearbox that drive the lift-fan. While not considered a show-stopper, this was the third problem with the STOVL system during preflight testing. The first delay came after the failure of a chipped gear and halted testing for a month in early 2000. Then the introduction of a different engine uncovered a vibration in the low-power turbine.

Engine testing began on June 11, 1998, on Test Stand A-9 at the Pratt & Whitney facility in West Palm Beach, Florida. These tests included component performance evaluations, compression system stability demonstrations, vibration surveys, operating system functional verification, and control software verification. The JSF119-611 engine was then instrumented for simulated altitude testing at the Air Force's Arnold Engineering Development Center (AEDC) in Tullahoma, Tennessee. The engine demonstrated component efficiencies higher than anticipated, turbine temperatures lower than predicted, and very low vibration levels. In addition, compression system stability margins and control software were verified.

The STOVL propulsion system had accumulated about 200 hours of hover testing by late June 2000, and the bearing problem was discovered after approximately 20 full-up clutch engagements out of the total 100 required. Lockheed had expected a standing-wave vibration problem where the shaft drive comes out of the engine, but the anomaly never materialized. The problems had been diagnosed and solved by midsummer 2000 when it was discovered that the bearing simply needed a break-in period before being run at high power. A few weeks later the clutch between the main engine and lift-fan failed during a test and renewed critics' claims that the system was too complicated and fragile, a claim Lockheed denies.

During late 1999, the Lockheed Martin JSF team demonstrated dramatic savings in airframe assembly time by using advanced design and manufacturing processes. The demonstration was conducted on a wing carry-through assembly during the first phase of the Aircraft Affordability Demonstration (AAD). This was part of a series of affordability and producibility demonstrations intended to reduce production cost and risk of the JSF program. The purpose of the AAD program is to demonstrate substantial savings in span times and man-hours in design, tooling, fabrication, and assembly of the JSF airframe. The structural assembly loading demonstration took less than one hour, compared to several days for this operation using traditional assembly methods. Tooling was reduced by 95 percent, and there were significant reductions in assembly man-hours. "The results of this demonstration show we are

Unlike many prototypes and demonstrators, the JSF aircraft were rolled out in standard Air Force tactical camouflage. Neither the X-32 nor X-35 carried any national insignia, a possible concession to their multinational potential? The Lockheed aircraft sport a red stripe with four "X"s—the normal Edwards flight test marking—on their vertical stabilizer. Otherwise, markings are limited to a JSF badge on each side of the aircraft. In some photos, a Pratt & Whitney logo has been added to the air intake. *Lockheed Martin Skunk Works photo by Denny Lombard*

The composite top fuselage from DarkStar was easily handled by two men to show how light the modern composites are. This also gives an indication of the size of DarkStar, which was not a small drone. The large rectangular opening is for the engine air intake and will be covered later during assembly. The openings behind the air intake will contain flush GPS, Ku-band, and UHF antennas. *Lockheed Martin Skunk Works*

on track with our plan to produce an affordable next-generation fighter," said Cappuccio. "We exceeded our program goals for the savings demonstrated, and we did so ahead of schedule and on budget."

"We are performing this demonstration using our Preferred Weapon System Concept design that we will be proposing next year, which is very similar to our X-35 concept demonstrator in structure. By building our X-35 concept demonstrator aircraft using traditional means and then demonstrating these new aircraft affordability processes, we have an excellent basis for comparison and validating our data and savings," Cappuccio added. "These facts clearly reflect the stability and maturity of the Lockheed Martin team's JSF design, a key element in program risk assessment."

The JSF production decision underwent a great deal of scrutiny during early and mid-2000. The main concern was whether a single winning contractor would be selected, or whether a single winning design would be selected and then competed annually between Boeing and Lockheed Martin (much like the AMRAAM contracts in the 1980s). There were arguments for both cases. Keeping both contractors as viable future competitors required that both maintain the ability to manufacture high-performance aircraft, and JSF is the only one on the horizon. A drawback is that the economics of maintaining two industrial sources would drive the cost of JSF unacceptably high. In the end, it appears that a single

The rollout of the first DarkStar on June 1, 1995, was theatrically staged, complete with fog and colored lights. Unfortunately for the audience, even when the fog had lifted and lights came on, there was little that could be seen from their seats since DarkStar sat so low to the ground. The audience was allowed to walk around the drone after the ceremonies. Skunk Works and Boeing had great hopes for the Tier III drone program, and had invested a great deal of time and company money into concepts for DarkStar. *Lockheed Martin Skunk Works*

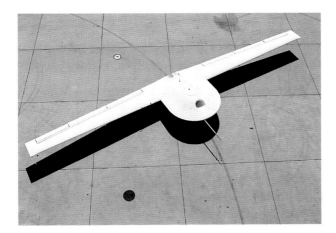

The unusual shape of the DarkStar is a tribute to modern computer design and automated flight control systems. The vehicle is essentially a long straight-wing with a short ogive fuselage, and doesn't have any vertical stabilizers. There were three trailing edge aerodynamic surfaces on each side of the wing, and these were used in various combinations to provide all pitch, yaw, and roll control. The forward air intake and rear slotted exhaust show up well here. *Lockheed Martin Skunk Works photo by Denny Lombard*

contractor will be selected sometime, although exactly when is less certain. Probably the new Bush administration will want time to review such a large program prior to making an announcement. In most probability, a final JSF contractor will not be selected before late 2001.

Tier III-(Minus)—RQ-3A DarkStar

The recent history of military unmanned aerial vehicles (UAVs, formerly called drones) has been confusing and unproductive. Despite spending a great deal of money on projects such as the Army's Aquila, few satisfactory operational systems have been fielded. Under provisions of the 1988 Intermediate-Range Nuclear Forces (INF) treaty, land-based unmanned aerial vehicles with a range of over 500 kilometers cannot be armed, which somewhat limits their usefulness.

In 1988, Congress directed the Department of Defense to develop a master plan for military UAVs. During the early 1990s, the DoD initiated an extremely ambitious and very expensive program to develop three tiers of UAVs to perform a wide variety of missions. These ranged from small expendable UAVs (Tier I – Hunter and Outrider), to very large, sophisticated platforms capable of performing all (or nearly all) the same missions as the U-2. In the end, $850 million in development funding couldn't overcome an alarmingly high projected unit cost for the original Tier III concept, and the project was canceled. In retrospect, the Air Force probably should have bought the U-2 RPV that Johnson had tried to sell them in 1974. The entire approach to UAVs was re-examined, and three vehicles emerged as part of the new Endurance UAV program originally managed by the DARPA Joint UAV Program Office for the Defense Airborne Reconnaissance Office (DARO).

The Medium Altitude Endurance (MAE) vehicle (Tier II) is known as the RQ-1A Predator, and has been operational with the air force since June 1996. This UAV weighs just under 2,000 pounds and has a nominal flight duration of 24 hours at a mission station approximately 500 nautical miles from its launch site. Predator's normal air speed is about 100 knots at an altitude of 15,000 feet. It can carry a 450-pound payload of primarily Synthetic Aperture Radar (SAR) and Electro-Optic/Infrared(EO/IR) sensors. The Air Force has recently been exploring the idea of arming the Predator, treaty restrictions notwithstanding.

The High Altitude Endurance (HAE) UAV is the RQ-4A Global Hawk built by Northrop Grumman, which acquired the original developer, Teledyne Ryan. In the new numbering scheme, this UAV was assigned Tier II+ (Plus). This is the mother of all UAVs. It boasts a wingspan of 116 feet and supports a gross weight of almost 25,000 pounds. The aircraft can cruise at 250 knots at altitudes over 65,000 feet, and has a 2,000-pound payload capacity consisting of both SAR and EO/IR sensors. With the SAR

The second DarkStar air vehicle during its second test flight on September 16, 1998. This was a very conservative flight and achieved a maximum altitude of only 5,000 feet. The arrangement of the control surfaces appears to be slightly different from the first vehicle, with a small nonmovable piece of the trailing edge between the outer split-aileron and the middle control surface. On the first air vehicle the three movable segments took up the entire trailing edge. *U.S. Air Force*

payload the Global Hawk can survey up to 40,000 square nautical miles per day per aircraft at better than 3-foot resolution or form 1,900 1-foot spot images, each one mile square, at 1-foot resolution.

Although it is assigned a higher Tier number, the Tier III- (Minus) RQ-3A DarkStar actually fits somewhere between the other two in capabilities. Known as the Low Observable High Altitude Endurance (LO-HAE), the development of this UAV was awarded to a team of Skunk Works and Boeing in early 1994 as a classified program. The Pentagon and industry sources have suggested that the DarkStar was a consolation prize awarded without publicity to Lockheed-Boeing after the much larger Tier III stealthy subsonic UAV program (also known as "Q") they were developing was canceled in 1992. That program, whose full name has never been formally revealed, was initiated in the early 1980s by the Central Intelligence Agency (CIA) with later participation by the Air Force.

Skunk Works was responsible for the design and development of DarkStar's body and subsystems, final assembly, and integration and system test, while Boeing designed and built the wing and wing subsystem development and test, and integration of the avionics and sensors. In 1996, the DarkStar program emerged from the black world. As part of the restructuring of the UAV programs, both Global Hawk and DarkStar were limited to

a maximum unit cost of $10 million (fiscal year [FY94] dollars). All other system attributes, including performance, were traded off against this requirement. The government defined this as "cost as an independent variable," and the intent was to arrive at a system solution which was not the best that could be imagined, but rather good enough to do the job, and inexpensive enough to make it through Congress.

The Tier III- program was the first project to be executed under the "Section 845 Authority" granted to DARPA for prototype weapons development. This authority paved the way for unprecedented government-industry collaboration by removing the burden of specialized Department of Defense procurement regulations. The DarkStar came with a one-page specification that simply specified best altitude, endurance, and signature for a $10-million unit cost for the second batch of 10 air vehicles. It was acknowledged that the first 10 vehicles might be more expensive before the experience in manufacturing them was gained.

The graphite composite DarkStar air vehicle combined high-aspect-ratio wings that had a slight degree of forward sweep with a short fuselage that resembled an archway with the top of the arch facing forward. Seen head-on, the fuselage's pronounced chine divided a rounded upper body from an almost flat underside. The wing's nearly unswept form reduced reflectivity spikes (high radar reflections) to two narrow sectors ahead and behind the aircraft, while the fuselage showed up as a "fuzz ball" of generally low reflectivity. The engine air intake was masked from below by the rest of the fuselage, and narrow ducts in the rear of the fuselage diffused the engine's infrared signature. Ku-band, UHF, and Global Positioning System (GPS) satellite antennas were located on top of the fuselage to mask them from the ground. The aircraft had a 69-foot wingspan, weighed 8,600 pounds, and used a single Williams International FJ44 turbofan engine. The DarkStar had a 1,000-pound payload and carried either a Northrop Grumman low-probability-of-intercept (LPI) SAR, or a Recon-Optical EO sensor. The DarkStar was supposed to operate at a range of 500 nautical miles from the launch site and be able to loiter over the target area for more than eight hours at an altitude of more than 45,000 feet.

The first DarkStar was rolled out on June 1, 1995, and made its maiden flight from Edwards AFB on March 29, 1996. During the 44-minute flight, the vehicle achieved an altitude of approximately 5,000 feet and completed pre-programmed basic flight maneuvers. The system successfully executed a fully autonomous flight from takeoff to landing utilizing a differential GPS. A second flight on April 21, 1996, resulted in the loss of the first DarkStar due to incorrect aerodynamic modeling of the vehicle's flight control laws. A known "wheel-barrowing" characteristic on its takeoff roll increased to uncontrollable "porpoising" (bobbing up and down) after leaving the ground, and the aircraft stalled nose-high and crashed.

Based on the conclusions of the accident investigation, Skunk Works modified the second air vehicle with new landing gear, redesigned the flight control software, and conducted extensive simulations prior to beginning taxi tests in March 1998. Prior to the second vehicle being modified

The careful blending of the air intake into the surrounding fuselage helped reduce the RCS of DarkStar. This is the second air vehicle, and shows the absolutely smooth surface made possible by the composite construction techniques. During the flight test program, both air vehicles were fitted with flight test data booms that protruded from the nose. *Lockheed Martin Skunk Works*

Only the outer control surface of the DarkStar was split to allow it to act as a speed brake and/or aileron. DarkStar had a 69-foot wingspan, weighed 8,600 pounds, and used a single Williams International FJ44 turbofan engine. The primary payload was either a Northrop Grumman low-probability-of-intercept (LPI) SAR or a Recon-Optical EO sensor. *Lockheed Martin Skunk Works photo by Denny Lombard*

It seems difficult to believe that such a straight-wing vehicle could be designed to have a low RCS, but Skunk Works pulled it off by carefully shaping the wing and the juncture with the fuselage. The air intake, engine exhaust, and all communications antennas were located on top of the vehicle to shield them from the ground. When the landing gear was tucked away and the ATC transponder turned off, about all that was visible from the bottom was the sensor port for the payload, and even this was constructed to minimize its RCS. *Lockheed Martin Skunk Works*

to serve in the flight test program, it was extensively "pole" tested at the Lockheed RCS measurement range beginning in May 1996 to verify its LO characteristics.

The second DarkStar made its maiden flight on June 29, 1998, and a second flight followed on September 16, 1998. Both flights reached a maximum altitude of 5,000 feet, sufficient for the flight test objectives, but low enough to ensure the vehicle could not crash anywhere except over the uninhabited dry lakes. On January 11, 1999, the second vehicle made its first high-altitude flight and reached 25,000 feet over Edwards. The 2-hour-and-37-minute flight included a demonstration of the ability to alter pre-programmed mission data while the vehicle was in flight.

Originally, both the Global Hawk and DarkStar were part of a four-phase program under the auspices of

DARPA: Phase I was the concept definition phase and resulted in the selection of Skunk Works and Teledyne Ryan to develop vehicles. Phase II focused on developing, fabricating, and flight-testing both systems. Testing was to include airworthiness and payload performance testing, as well as some limited field demonstrations. As originally planned, two Global Hawks, four DarkStars, and one common ground station were to be built and tested during Phase II, which was expected to run through September 1998. Phase III intended to focus on operational demonstration and user evaluation of the two systems through field demonstrations and military exercises. During this phase, scheduled to run through September 2000, additional air vehicles and common ground stations were to be built. The completion of Phase III was to be followed by a decision whether to enter into full production in Phase IV.

The Air Force assumed the management of both Global Hawk and DarkStar in late 1998 and finally wrestled the program away from DARPA and its research origins. The change in management had always been expected, but at some point later in the development cycle than when it occurred. Almost immediately the Air Force attempted to change the basic capabilities of both UAVs. This was a detriment to both programs and resulted in an investigation by the Congressional Budget Office (CBO), which came to a surprising conclusion. The CBO decided that additional Global Hawks could substitute for the much more expensive E-8 JSTARS, and that the DarkStar program should be canceled. The three completed Dark-Stars would be used as "silver bullets" for operations against extremely valuable and well-defended targets.

This report, along with the changing political climate, brought a different set of needs, and the crash of the first DarkStar irreversibly damaged the program's chances of success. On January 26, 1999, the Department of Defense canceled the DarkStar program due to budget cuts. Given a tradeoff between stealth and range, the air force chose the range of Global Hawk over DarkStar's stealth, and Skunk Work's second drone program came to an end. Other fallout from these actions was that DARPA went out of the UAV business, and DARO was disbanded.

At the time, the second air vehicle had completed five successful flights, the third air vehicle had completed ground checks and was ready to be delivered for flight testing, the fourth flight vehicle was undergoing ground tests, and the fifth flight vehicle was in final assembly. The remaining funds from the original $20-million FY00 allocation for DarkStar were transferred to complete production of five Global Hawks and purchase an additional ground station. The Air Force subsequently decided that the DarkStars "were too fragile to be used operationally," and the vehicles were placed in storage. Skunk Works, never without something up its sleeve, is at work on various UAV projects ranging from hand-sized micro-aircraft to full-size unmanned combat aircraft.

The X-35A during its first flight on October 24, 2000. Lockheed Martin test pilot Tom Morgenfield was at the controls. The flight lifted off from the main runway at Palmdale and flew to nearby Edwards AFB. The unique configuration of the horizontal stabilizers shows up well in this photo. Notice that the hinge line is even with the engine nozzle. *Lockheed Martin Aeronautics Company*

Above: This is the carrier-capable X-35C demonstrator at Palmdale. Besides the larger wing, the most prominent change is the tail hook under the rear fuselage. Surprisingly, the tail hook isn't completely retractable on the X-35, although if probably will be on production JSFs in order to maintain stealth. A stylized Lockheed Martin JSF logo is on the side of the fuselage just behind the cockpit. *Lockheed Martin Skunk Works*

Right: The X-35A takes fuel from a KC-135 tanker on November 7, 2000, marking the JSF's first in-flight refueling. Lt. Col. Paul Smith took off from Edwards AFB, climbed to 23,000 feet, and executed four refueling events. The 2 hour and 50 minute flight was the longest yet for the conventional takeoff and landing (CTOL) X-35A. About two weeks after this photo was taken, the aircraft was returned to Palmade to be converted into the STOVL demonstrator. The lift-fan was installed under the doors seen directly behind the pilot. *Lockheed Martin Aeronautics Company*

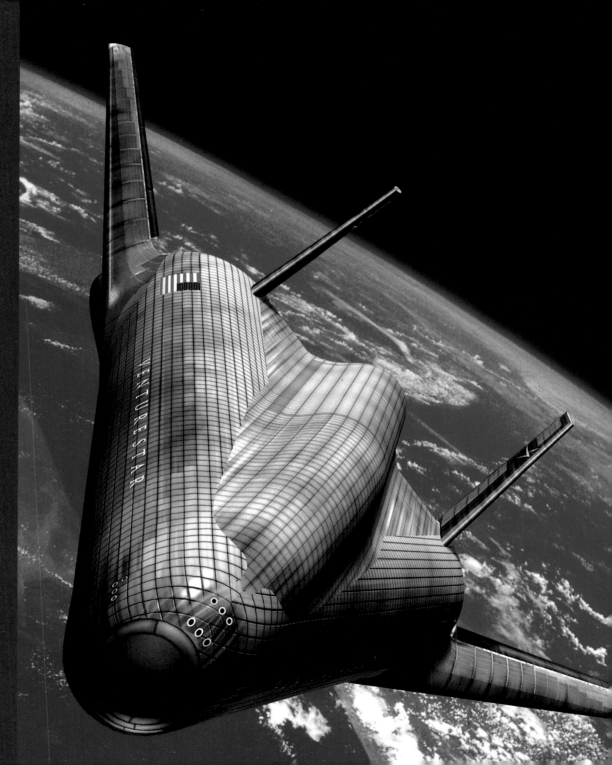

Five

The payload is beginning to be moved outside of the basic vehicle in this early-2000 concept for VentureStar. By mid-2000 the payload had been moved completely out of the vehicle and into a piggyback container. This may not be detrimental since it would allow the vehicle to carry payloads of almost any given size and shape, at least within some aerodynamic and thermal considerations. In this drawing it appears that the entire topside of the vehicle is covered with metallic heat shields instead of the blankets that were expected to be used. The Skunk Works logos on the vertical stabilizers have been replaced with Lockheed Martin star logos, probably to signify the increased corporate emphasis placed on the program. *Lockheed Martin Skunk Works*

Countdown to VentureStar™ —*THE X-33*

In what is perhaps the most exciting project Skunk Works approached during the 1990s, the company left their "black" origins far behind and elected to tackle one of the most visible NASA programs of the decade. Unfortunately this also meant that many of the traditional Skunk Works philosophies could not be applied to the project, which has run into tremendous technical and managerial difficulties.

Clarification

Before we get too far, it should be noted that there is a popular misconception (aided by Lockheed Martin public relations who puts both X-33 and VentureStar™ logos on everything) that the X-33 is named VentureStar. This is not the case. VentureStar is the name of the commercial Reusable Launch Vehicle (RLV) that may result from a successful X-33 flight test program. The X-33 is a 53-percent scale model of that vehicle. There is a misconception that the X-33 is a single-stage-to-orbit (SSTO) vehicle, and again, this is not the case. The X-33 is an exo-atmospheric flight test vehicle incapable of achieving orbit. The goal of the X-33 flight test program is to demonstrate key SSTO technologies and operational concepts. A careful analysis of these technologies and concepts showed that it was unnecessary and expensive to build an orbital vehicle. The X-33's performance is sufficient to demonstrate all aspects necessary to create an operational SSTO RLV.

For about 30 years, almost all major aerospace companies around the world, including Skunk Works and other Lockheed organizations, have investigated the possibility of reusable spacecraft.

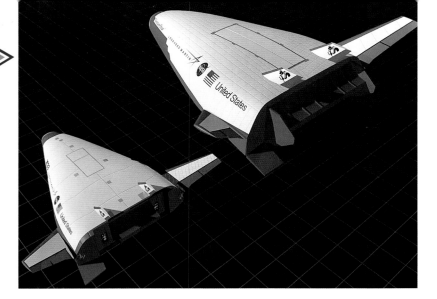

When the Skunk Works program was approved in 1996, this was the relationship between the X-33 demonstrator and the eventual VentureStar RLV. The X-33 was a 53 percent scale version of the VentureStar intended to test many of the technologies required for a SSTO vehicle. At this point in time the two vehicles looked extremely similar, except X-33 used only two engines while VentureStar had seven. This similarity would begin to change as the program continued. *Lockheed Martin Skunk Works drawing by John Frassanito & Associates, Inc.*

The Lockheed X-Rocket of 1988 was a SSTO vehicle that looked remarkably like the McDonnell Douglas DC-X Delta Clipper (Clipper Graham). Lockheed envisioned a conical vehicle that would launch and land vertically, and was 60 feet tall and 34 feet in diameter. This vehicle was one of a series of design studies conducted by Skunk Works that eventually led to the VentureStar program. *Lockheed Martin Skunk Works*

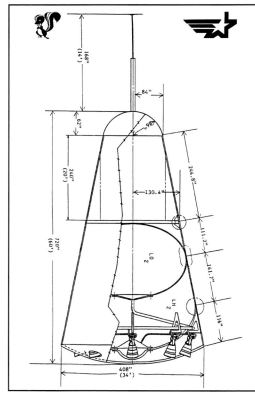

Some of the more notable Lockheed studies included the stage-and-a-half stage StarClipper (1965–1968), the Space Shuttle Phase A and B concepts (1965–1969), the wing-body SSTO Trans-Atmospheric Vehicle (TAV) (1983–1988), and the conical SSTO X-Rocket (1988).

Unlike traditional rockets and the space shuttle, all of which throw away various parts of their structure on the way to orbit, an SSTO vehicle operates very much like a normal aircraft; sort of. The idea for an SSTO has been around for a long time. Eugen Sänger wrote of them during the 1920s, and people have been trying to figure out how to make them work ever since. The Air Force attempted to design several during the 1950s, 1960s, and 1970s. The nation as a whole attempted to design the National Aero-Space Plane (NASP, or the X-30) during the 1980s and early 1990s. The British, Germans, Japanese, and Soviets have also tried. All of these efforts failed.

There was a common reason for the failure: getting an object into orbit is hard. The vehicle has to accelerate to 17,000 miles per hour, and by most definitions, an SSTO vehicle needs to carry all of its propellants with it. It also has to be able to take off, fly in the atmosphere, orbit, survive re-entry, and land. The vehicle has to be stable at Mach 25 to achieve orbit, and also be stable at 200 knots in order to land. It has to be capable of surviving the incredible temperatures of atmospheric re-entry, yet have a structure that is extremely lightweight and durable. The engines must be powerful enough to accelerate the vehicle to Mach 25, yet be efficient enough to allow it to carry sufficient propellants. The creation of a workable SSTO will require many break-through technologies, mainly in the areas of highly efficient rocket engines, lightweight structures, and advanced control systems.

NASA has been looking at concepts to replace the Space Shuttle almost since the beginning of the operational era in 1983. The experience with the shuttle has not been a completely happy one. Initially the program was aimed to dramatically reduce the cost of access to space by employing a completely reusable two-stage-to-orbit (TSTO) vehicle. In concept, a TSTO vehicle should be easier to design and build than an SSTO. In practice, it presents almost as many challenges, and budgetary restrictions forced NASA to abandon the concept for the shuttle and settle for a sort of "stage-and-a-half" vehicle where some parts are thrown away during each mission.

Although the stage-and-a-half vehicle greatly reduced the cost of initially developing the shuttle, it significantly increased the cost and complexity of operating the vehicle. In addition, the technology available in the 1970s while the shuttle was being designed led to the development of a fairly conventional aluminum vehicle covered with a thermal protection system. The advanced composite materials that are common today were just beginning to be applied in small amounts at the time. The ceramic thermal protection tiles used on the shuttle were a marvelous invention when they were developed, but they have proven to be very fragile and labor intensive in actual operations. All of this resulted in a grand experiment that has not lived up to its expectations, although the shuttle represents a magnificent first attempt.

The cancellation of the truly ambitious NASP in 1990 resulted in NASA embarking on a series of studies of possible ways to lower the cost of access to space. Along the way, NASA cooperated with the air force in evaluating the Douglas DC-X (also called the Delta

Clipper and Clipper Graham). The basic goals of any eventual RLV sounded a lot like those originally applied to the shuttle program: routine and low-cost access to space. Unlike in the 1960s when a TSTO vehicle was the preferred concept, by the 1990s, most studies were concentrating on SSTO designs.

Like most things in life, designing an SSTO vehicle can take several approaches. The most noticeable parameter is the attitude used during launch and landing. The DC-X had demonstrated the "vertical takeoff and vertical landing" (VTVL) mode. Either mode could, in theory, also be horizontal and more like a conventional aircraft. This leads to four possibilities: VTVL, VTHL, HTVL, and HTHL. Not surprisingly, almost nobody ever proposes the horizontal takeoff and vertical landing (HTVL) mode.

The Competition

In 1993 NASA conducted the "Access to Space" study and concluded that a fully reusable SSTO launch system offered the best approach to achieving a truly affordable launch capability. Unlike other recent space transportation studies, "Access to Space" resulted in a program that was initiated to do something about the situation. NASA began a competition to build an RLV technology demonstrator, and three industry teams submitted very different designs. McDonnell Douglas submitted a larger variation of their VTVL DC-X, Rockwell International offered a fairly conventional appearing HTHL vehicle, and Skunk Works submitted a VTHL design that resurrected the "lifting-body" shape that had been investigated by NASA and the air force during the 1960s.

On July 2, 1996, Vice President Al Gore announced that Lockheed Martin had been selected to lead a government-industry partnership to design and flight-test the X-33 demonstrator. Notice that this was not a contract award *per se*; it is technically a Cooperative Agreement (NCC-8-73) and NASA is a teammate and not a customer. The X-33 program would demonstrate

X-24C

As the X-15 project came to a close in the late 1960s, there were many suggestions for a follow-on to the project. One of these suggestions was generally called the X-24C, although a variety of different concepts were investigated under this designation. The Air Force studies usually emphasized configurations suitable for military missions such as reconnaissance, while the NASA designs were more applicable to long-range hypersonic transports.

As late as July 1974, NASA and the Air Force jointly conducted a series of conceptual studies exploring various options for an air-breathing hypersonic aircraft. A realization that surfaced from these studies was that the FDL-8 (X-24B) shape appeared ideal. Two versions of this configuration, one with dual cheek-type air intakes for supersonic jet engines and the other powered by a modified version of the XLR99, were released for comment in late 1974. NASA and the air force subsequently established the "X-24C Joint Steering Committee," which promptly rejected the relatively conservative vehicles proposed by NASA and the Air Force Flight Dynamics Laboratory (AFFDL), and started forming its own conclusions about the future of hypersonic research.

Out of this committee came the National Hypersonic Flight Research Facility (NHFRF – pronounced "nerf") concept in July 1975. NASA forecast a $200-million program involving construction of two aircraft with 200 flights over a 10-year period. NASA and the air force would start funding the program in 1980 with the first flight in 1983. Initially the vehicle was built upon the proven X-24B shape, but as the program became steadily more ambitious, NHFRF slowly began to change itsconfiguration.

The NHFRF vehicle would have a top speed of Mach 8, with an extended Mach 6 cruise. One of the primary areas of research envisioned for the vehicle was advanced propulsion systems such as scramjets. During preliminary studies, several of the designs that were proposed by various manufacturers bore more than a passing resemblance to the final Aerospaceplane configurations from the early 1960s. After reviewing the preliminary studies, NASA selected Skunk Works to conduct a detailed analysis and preliminary design with the probability that they would eventually build the vehicles.

The study that Skunk Works conducted was exhaustive and ran from November 1975 until at least January 1977, and possibly continued after this date. Initially Harry Combs and his Skunk Works team focused on defining a feasible propulsion system for the hypersonic vehicle. It was obvious that rocket engines provided the only reasonable means of achieving the desired speeds, but the 40-second steady state Mach 6 cruise required much lower thrust than the initial acceleration, and thus led to the concept of using separate cruise engines.

Engines that were considered during the study included extended-nozzle XLR99s, XLR11s, Rocketdyne LR105 sustainer engines from the Atlas ICBM, and LR101 vernier engines from the same missile. The problem was illustrated by the fact that either the XLR99 or LR105 was necessary to provide the initial speed increment, but the effort to sustain Mach 6 cruise and a dynamic pressure of 1,000 pounds per square foot at 90,000 feet required only 16,000 pounds-thrust. Under those conditions the minimum thrust from the XLR99 was 29,500 pounds-thrust. The LR105 was even worse at 46,000 pounds-thrust. Without separate cruise engines, this feat would have required the use of speed brakes during the entire cruise portion of flight, leading to higher propellant consumption and some interesting structural heating problems.

As with all proposals for air-launched vehicles using the NB-52 aircraft, the X-24C/NHFRF was limited to 57,000 pounds. To achieve the weight requirement, Skunk Works proposed Lockalloy as the major structural material. The entire skin area, including leading edges, was made of a sufficient thickness of Lockalloy to act as a heat sink and not require the use of a thermal protection system. However, some mention

The final X-24C design from Skunk Works had migrated away from a true lifting-body design and included a large integrated scramjet engine on the lower fuselage. In addition, a single large rocket engine (probably an LR105 from the Atlas ICBM) was located in the rear fuselage to accelerate the vehicle to a speed where the scramjet could be ignited. At this time it was widely expected that any future operational hypersonic aircraft would use scramjet engines. *Tony Landis Collection*

was made in the study of the possible use of LI-900 tiles (a variation of what was eventually used on the space shuttle) in very high heat areas.

During 1977 the estimated costs of NHFRF escalated past $500 million, and led NASA Headquarters to cancel the effort in September 1977. NASA acting Associate Administrator for Aeronautics and Space Technology James J. Kramer stated that, "the combination of a tight budget and the inability to identify a pressing near-term need for the flight facility had led to a decision by NASA not to proceed with a flight test vehicle at this time." This was exactly the same rationale that had caused the demise of Dyna-Soar 10 years earlier.

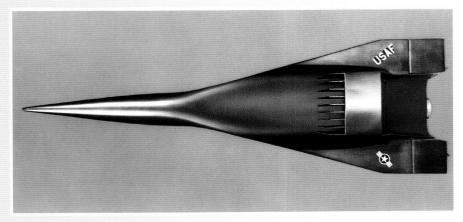

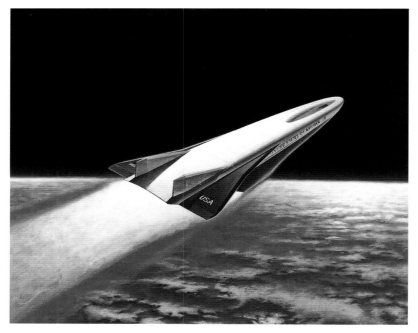

During the late 1950s and early 1960s, the Air Force had attempted to design an SSTO vehicle called Aerospace-plane. During the late 1980s and early 1990s, DARPA, NASA, and the Air Force tried again with the National Aero-Space Plane (NASP). This was the final design for the X-30 demonstrator that was intended to test the technologies necessary for NASP. This drawing was released on October 24, 1990. NASP would be canceled soon thereafter because it had become too expensive to develop. *Dennis R. Jenkins Collection*

advanced technologies intended to dramatically increase launch vehicle reliability and lower the cost of putting a pound of payload into space from $10,000 to $1,000. NASA committed to contributing $941 million for the X-33 program, while Lockheed Martin and its industry partners committed to invest at least $287 million. The government's share was supposed to be fixed, and any overruns were to be paid by the industry team.

The decision to select Skunk Works took most knowledgeable observers by surprise. It was widely expected that the overgrown DC-X would be selected since it had already garnered a good bit of publicity during earlier tests. While the publicity was priceless and some control-law development was shown, the DC-X had demonstrated very little of the hard technology needed to get to orbit. The Skunk Works design had been considered the back runner for two reasons: The first was the use of the lifting-body design. Although tests during the 1960s had demonstrated lifting-bodies were a viable concept throughout the speed range necessary to get to orbit, their constantly curving shape made packaging all the necessary items (such as large propellant tanks) inside the vehicle very difficult. The second reason was that Skunk Works had proposed a linear aerospike engine, a concept that had never been popular within NASA, and had been specifically banned from the shuttle competition 20 years earlier.

Perhaps one of the reasons NASA selected the Skunk Works entry was the apparent Lockheed commitment to the design. The X-33 was proposed as a half-scale prototype of a commercially developed RLV called VentureStar. NASA will be a customer, not the operator, of the VentureStar.

Lockheed's commitment played directly into the hands of NASA, who announced that one of the goals of the X-33 program was to provide a high level of confidence in the new technologies so industry could take the next step and independently finance, develop, build, and operate a full-scale RLV. Such a vehicle holds the promise of opening a new era in space transportation and will provide the United States a competitive advantage in launching commercial payloads and supporting the International Space Station (ISS).

Concept Evolution

In the beginning, Skunk Works focused their attention on designing the final VentureStar vehicle and always intended the X-33 to be a subscale prototype of whatever design emerged. Various mission concepts were evaluated early in the conceptual stage and a VTHL concept was selected because there was significant operational knowledge on this approach. In addition, horizontal landing seemed to better facilitate horizontal processing and aircraft-like operations. The studies concluded that a capability to deliver approximately 40,000 pounds into low-earth orbit (LEO) was sufficient to satisfy future Department of Defense, NASA, and commercial missions. A good deal of the final business case for developing VentureStar rested on it securing most of the resupply missions to the ISS.

These evaluations also concluded that a lifting-body was superior to either the wing-body (space shuttle) or the conical (DC-X) VTVL SSTO concepts, or the TSTO approach. The lifting-body offered the potential to eliminate the parasitic add-ons of the other configurations (wings) and had superior volumetric efficiency, aerodynamic stability, and aerothermodynamic characteristics to either of the other configurations.

Many of the original shuttle studies from the late 1960s and early 1970s had also concluded that the lifting-body was a desirable shape, and partially explained why so many different lifting-bodies were built and flight-tested. However, when it came to figuring out how to package all of the systems necessary for an operational vehicle, the lifting-body quickly became less desirable. One of the biggest drawbacks was how to package propellant tanks into the lifting-body shape. Without modern computers, it was difficult to calculate the distributed pressures inside a multi-lobe tank. Until the advent of modern metal alloys and composite materials, it was nearly impossible to build a lightweight multi-lobe cryogenic tank. It is also difficult to manufacture metal propellant tanks in complex shapes, and the lifting-body presented an extremely odd shape to

This is a fairly early X-33 design, although it is unusual in that the names of all the industrial partners are not emblazoned on the fuselage. One of the primary technologies that will be demonstrated by X-33 is a new TPS that will replace the tiles used on the space shuttle. These tiles have proven to be very maintenance intensive, and the X-33 will pioneer the use of a removable metallic heat shield on the bottom of the vehicle. The top of the fuselage will be covered by thermal blankets very similar to those used on the shuttle since these have proven very effective. *Lockheed Martin Skunk Works drawing by John Frassanito & Associates, Inc.*

package efficiently. Skunk Works believed that it had finally become possible to build oddly shaped, multi-lobe cryogenic propellant tanks.

The exact route to this conclusion was torturous. During the Assured Crew Return Vehicle (ACRV)

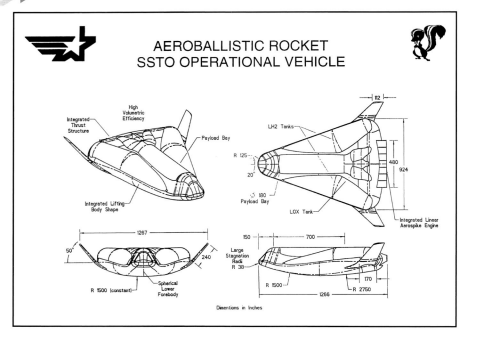

AEROBALLISTIC ROCKET
SSTO OPERATIONAL VEHICLE

The K-10 design (also called the Aeroballistic Rocket, or ABR) was the final evolution of the Lockheed SSTO concept before the L-1, which was the first VentureStar design. This vehicle shows most of the eventual configuration items included in VentureStar including an integrated thrust structure, seven linear aerospike engines, and large LH2 tanks on the outside of the payload bay. At this point the outer mold line of the upper body largely followed the structural components underneath it with no attempt at aerodynamic smoothing. This would be the major change made as the design progressed to the L-1 configuration and a smooth outer mold line was adopted. *Lockheed Martin Skunk Works*

study, Skunk Works engineers discovered that by combining large forebody radii of curvature with a smooth toroidal extension on the windward aeroshell, a significant improvement in the hypersonic lift-to-drag ratio could be realized. Static and dynamic stability for this shape could be realized with small control surfaces. This was in line with the original lifting-body studies done in the 1960s.

The work on the ACRV program was the genesis of the Skunk Works SSTO design. The initial VentureStar design concepts drew heavily upon the lessons learned from the ACRV and HL-20 design studies. The first lifting-body RLV concepts resembled a Boston Whaler boat and incorporated the ACRV large round nose, deep hull, and straight sides. Conformal propellant tanks were used for the primary load-bearing structure, and relatively cool re-entry temperatures enabled the use of a metallic thermal protection system (TPS). The payload bay nested between the propellant tanks and was partially exposed on the leeward surface for accessibility.

An aerodynamic analysis on the ACRV concluded that the vehicle would never balance throughout the flight envelope with the weight of the required rocket engines at the back. The logical solution was to reduce the area forward of the center of gravity and incorporate a swept platform reminiscent of the lifting-bodies developed during the 1960s. This led to the K-4 configuration that incorporated lighter semi-exposed conical LH2 tanks and an aft multi-lobe LO2 tank. Although the semi-exposed tanks were light, Navier-Stokes CFD aerodynamic analysis predicted a significant flow separation in the channel between the tanks and the payload bay. A smooth outer mold line was added over the entire top of the vehicle. Further refinements led to the L-1 baseline proposed to NASA.

During the ACRV's development, Skunk Works concluded that the linear aerospike engine offered the highest performance and lowest risk of any of the advanced RLV propulsion concepts. The engine also helped ease the center-of-gravity problems since an aerospike engine is significantly lighter than a traditional bell engine. The original aerospike engine was developed by Rocketdyne to support the Chrysler SERV Alternate Space Shuttle Concept, and was ground-tested in the late 1960s and early 1970s. Two advantages of the aerospike engine are the inherent altitude compensation afforded by the "inside out" nozzle and higher installed thrust-to-weight ratio.

Phase II

Phase I of the RLV program was the original competition. Phase II is the design, construction, and flight-testing of the X-33 vehicle. This phase originally had an ambitious schedule. The first flight of the X-33 vehicle was originally scheduled for March 1999, with the entire flight program due to end in December 1999. Unfortunately, this was not a feasible time frame.

There were three major goals of the Phase II program: The first of these was to demonstrate the most critical key technologies needed to achieve SSTO flight using the X-33. The second goal was the development and ground testing of the items not to be flown in the X-33, including a full-scale prototype of the RLV linear aerospike engine; a non-flight-rated unlined graphite-composite LO2 tank sized to fit in the X-33; cycle testing of an X-33 graphite/epoxy LH2 tank; and cycle, impact, and damage testing of the proposed VentureStar thermal protection system. The third goal was to continue the system definition, and optimize the full-scale Venture-Star vehicle and ground support system.

The X-33 began life essentially as a scale model of VentureStar and is similar in size to the F-117A stealth fighter. The X-33 design was frozen fairly early out of necessity so that the vehicle could be manufactured in time for the flight tests. Although it is 53 percent of the operational RLV's size, it has only 12.5 percent of the operational RLV's gross liftoff weight since it is not an orbital vehicle. At the time the X-33 design was frozen, the X-33 had the same internal arrangement and technology envisioned for VentureStar with one exception: the X-33 would use an aluminum-lithium 2195 alloy LO2 tank instead of the graphite-composite LO2 tank baselined for VentureStar.

The original flight test program was to begin in March 1999 and consisted of 15 flights at speeds up to Mach 15. The vehicle was never intended for orbital flight, but Mach 15 was chosen since the maximum aerodynamic pressure and temperature is encountered around this speed, and it is also about the maximum that can reasonably be achieved in the atmosphere. The velocity was considered sufficient to evaluate the RLV aerodynamics including real gas effects, the re-entry aerothermal environment, and to validate the metallic TPS design. All launches were to be from Edwards AFB, although the exact location changed several times based on various archeological and environmental considerations.

In November 1996, the X-33 program finally selected a launch site located at Area 1-56 near Haystack Butte on Edwards AFB. This location is approximately 15 miles across the lakebed from the NASA Dryden Flight Research Center, and is technically part of the Phillips Laboratory. The site was undeveloped, and a purpose-built launch pad was constructed by Sverdrup for X-33 use. An Operations Control Center is located in an underground bunker on Haystack Butte that was originally constructed in 1963 for a high-thrust rocket experiment that used facilities on the other side of the butte. Three landing sites were identified: Silurain Lake, just north of Baker, California; Michael Army Air Field, Utah; and Malmstrom AFB, Montana. Further simulation showed that the short-range low-speed (Mach 7 or 8) flights were to be used to prove the basic X-33 flight characteristics were unworkable, and Silurain was abandoned as a landing site.

One of the questions faced early in the project was how to get the X-33 back from its landing sites. The original plan was to use one of the Boeing 747 Shuttle Carrier Aircraft that are used to transport space shuttle

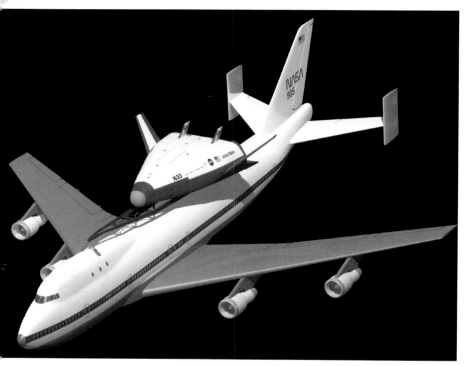

Early in the X-33 program, engineers pondered how to return the vehicle from the remote landing sites in Utah and Montana where the high-speed test flights were held. The most obvious answer was to use one of the 747 Shuttle Carrier Aircraft belonging to NASA. A study was accomplished that showed very few changes would be necessary. The X-33 would be carried on a cradle attached to the normal space shuttle points on the 747. There were people within NASA who were less than thrilled with this idea, and eventually it was decided to simply put the X-33 on a large truck and drive it back to the Edwards launch site. *National Aeronautics and Space Administration*

orbiters. A preliminary design of a cradle that allowed the X-33 to use the same mounting locations was developed, although certain considerations still required minor modifications to the 747. The Space Shuttle Program was not thrilled at the prospect of one of its 747s being modified and balked at the concept. In June 1998, Skunk Works finally conceded and began planning to transport the X-33 overland by a truck from the landing sites back to Edwards. The X-33 is being manufactured in the Boeing North American B-1 facility located at Air Force Plant 42, Site 7, in Palmdale. This is across the runway from the shuttle manufacturing site, and just east of the main Skunk Works facility at Site 10.

The X-33

The X-33 demonstrator incorporates many of the new technologies needed to build an SSTO vehicle, and will evaluate the performance of these technologies as an integrated flight system. To reduce weight, many structural elements are being manufactured with lightweight graphite-composite materials. The vehicle utilizes state-of-the-art avionics, and all crew life-support systems are eliminated since the vehicle is not piloted. It should be noted that VentureStar is also not a piloted vehicle, and crew members for the ISS will be carried in a passenger compartment installed in place of the payload module.

The lower exterior surface of the X-33 will be covered by 1,241 Inconel-617 and Titanium-1100 metallic TPS panels, while the leading edges and nose cap will be carbon-carbon, very similar to material used on the space shuttle orbiter. In order to minimize costs, X-33 will use an upper surface composed of graphite-composite panels covered with an AFRSI blanket insulation in lieu of the Titanium-1100 panels scheduled for use on VentureStar. Internal temperatures during re-entry should not exceed 350 degrees Fahrenheit, while external surfaces will heat up to temperatures between 1,600 and 2,200 degrees Fahrenheit. By comparison, the shuttle is equipped with approximately 24,000 ceramic tiles that are brittle and prone to damage, plus 3,000 blankets. Some 17,000 labor-hours are required to inspect, replace, and waterproof the shuttle tiles after each mission.

The X-33 will be powered by two Rocketdyne J-2S-based RS-2200 linear aerospike engines, each having two thrust cells. Steering is accomplished by varying the thrust of individual thrust cells instead of the heavy gimbal system used by conventional rocket engines. At full fuel load, the X-33 has a liftoff thrust-to-weight ratio of 1.5:1 and has been designed to continue flying with one engine out. At partial fuel loads, the combination of a high liftoff thrust-to-weight ratio and a 120 percent emergency power rating allows the X-33 to survive an engine out at liftoff.

Conventional rocket engines use a "bell nozzle" to contain their thrust, and this is good and bad. It is good because it is a well-understood technology, but the use of a fixed-size nozzle limits the flexibility of the engine dramatically. A bell nozzle designed to work well at sea-level pressure does work well in the vacuum of near-space, and vice versa. The bell tends to be very heavy and usually requires a complex regenerative cooling system. The aerospike engine overcomes this by using the atmosphere itself as the outer walls of the nozzle and allows the design to automatically adjust to changing atmospheric conditions as the vehicle climbs to orbit, and enhances its efficiency throughout ascent. Linear aerospike engines are 75 percent smaller than bell-nozzle rocket engines of comparable thrust. The smaller design means less engine weight and engine support structure required, which allows for a lighter spacecraft.

Despite the engines' improved efficiency and lighter weight, at times measures were considered to further improve the performance of the RS-2200 engines. During the summer of 1997, engineers looked into the feasibility of using "slush" or "near-slush" hydrogen instead of liquid hydrogen. Slush hydrogen is a colder and more dense propellant that contains more energy per cubic volume, and would have eased some of the performance

penalty the X-33 encountered because it continued to be overweight. A great deal of research had been conducted on slush hydrogen as part of the NASP program during the 1980s, but no major production facilities existed and only limited operational experience had been gained. In the end the complications outweighed the slight performance advantages, and the idea was dropped.

To save time and money for the demonstrator, Lockheed and Rocketdyne proposed using the turbo-machinery from the J-2S engines used on the Saturn V as a basis for their linear aerospike, and sufficient quantities of J-2S spares were still in storage at the NASA Marshall Space Flight Center. The adaptation of the J-2S machinery to the RS-2200 ran into trouble early on and resulted in delays. Fortunately performance estimates did not change. The RS-2200 test program finally began on October 2, 1998, with a 2.81-second test intended to calibrate instrumentation on the turbopumps. On October 27, 1998, Skunk Works announced that the delays encountered by the engine would force a six-month slip in the first flight. Surprisingly the composite hydrogen tank was not mentioned, although it represented as much, or perhaps more, of a pacing item to the flight test program.

Once engine testing got underway, it progressed rapidly. On November 24, 1998, an engine ran to 57 percent power. By January 13, the engine had completed a 250-second partial-power test. The four flight-rated engines were officially rolled out on July 6, 1999. The first two engines were dedicated to ground testing and flight certification testing, while the other two are the flight engines that will power the X-33. If necessary the two ground-test engines can be refurbished and installed on the vehicle.

On December 18, 1999, the first RS-2200 was run at 100 percent power for the first time during an 18-second test at Stennis. Minor problems were uncovered, but confidence was high that they could be overcome quickly. The engines were up to 60-second runs by the end of January 2000 and had successfully demonstrated the thrust vectoring capability

The X-33 begins to come together in Building 704 at Palmdale. This Air Force building is usually controlled by Boeing and was being used for modifications to B-1B bombers as the X-33 program got started. The large double-lobed liquid oxygen tank is being installed in the nose, and the empty space behind it is where the composite liquid hydrogen tanks will be installed, assuming they can ever be manufactured successfully. *Lockheed Martin Skunk Works photo by Marty Wolin*

necessary to control the X-33 during ascent. A 125-second test at 100 percent power was accomplished on February 3, 2000, and included extensive thrust vectoring. A minor setback occurred on March 9 when the engine prematurely shut down after only 75.44 seconds of a planned 220-second run. The shutdown was attributed to a software error that was quickly corrected. Two weeks later the engine completed a 220-second test, and finally demonstrated a full-length 250-second (250.02 to be exact) test at 100 percent power on April 6. There were no anomalies or engine problems encountered.

One of the conclusions from the DC-X demonstration program was that it should not take a standing army to operate a launch vehicle. Almost 18,000 workers are employed to maintain and operate the space shuttle fleet, and it takes 60 to 70 days to prepare a shuttle for a new mission. By contrast, the X-33 will require only about 50 people and have a 48-hour turnaround, and the VentureStar will require under 300 people and have a turnaround of less than one week. NASA and industry estimate the cost for each flight of a full-scale RLV will be about one-tenth as much as the space shuttle, or roughly $50 million each.

On October 31, 1997, the X-33 successfully passed its Critical Design Review. The five-day event was attended by over 590 people who were presented with over 2,750 charts in 11 volumes that detailed the progress made on the project to date. This milestone allowed Lockheed Martin to begin assembling the flight vehicle.

The First Delays

Despite the promise of a quick and efficient Skunk Works–type development effort, the large number of teammates and requirements for complete documentation and coordination quickly resulted in a bureaucracy Skunk Works was unfamiliar with. On June 24, 1997, Skunk Works announced that "typical development problems" would delay the beginning of flight testing from March to July 1999. The primary problem was a delay in the fabrication of the liquid hydrogen tank, something that proved to be the pacing item for the next three years.

Similar to the space shuttle, the X-33 will use liquid oxygen and liquid hydrogen as propellants. Originally, the X-33's hydrogen tank was to be manufactured from advanced graphite-composite materials. A key technology requirement for VentureStar was that only composite tanks could be shaped in such a manner to fit into the original continuously curving lifting-body. The confidence level was sufficiently high that designers intended to manufacture all of VentureStar's propellant tanks from composites as well, although the X-33 was always going to use an aluminum oxygen tank. This technology would prove elusive.

Almost from the beginning, the composite hydrogen tanks presented manufacturing problems. On July 22, 1998, it was announced that the delivery of the two X-33 tanks had each slipped about 45 days, with the first tank scheduled to be delivered to Palmdale on September 2. On September 27 the tanks had still not arrived due to continuing manufacturing problems, which resulted in another 30-day delay. It was not until October 28, 1998, that both hydrogen tanks were structurally completed. Now they had to be tested.

After testing began, it was immediately noted that there were bubbles and cracks in the skin lobes on one tank. Further examination revealed that the entire skin on the first tank was flawed. The flaws were so extensive that the skin had to be removed, and a new skin was manufactured and bonded to the structure. On January 21, 1999, Skunk Works announced another slip in the launch schedule. July 2000 was the date given to allow time to recover from the hydrogen tank problems. At the same time, the first tank suffered more damage when an internal wall failed during a heat treatment cycle. The damage to the tank was estimated at $5 million.

Fortunately, the aluminum oxygen tanks were doing better. On May 7, 1999, the two weeks of testing on the structural test article of the oxygen tank were successfully completed, but the hydrogen tanks were still having problems. On October 15, 1999, 34 major leaks were discovered in the second tank, and further problems were encountered over the next couple of weeks. On November 4, NASA announced that "damage was discovered Wednesday [November 3] evening to one wall of the X-33 composite liquid hydrogen tank currently undergoing cryogenic and structural loads testing at NASA Marshall Space Flight Center." The outer skin and honeycomb center had pulled away from the inner lining. A high-level failure investigation board was convened, and Congress became involved with special committees. The investigation would last for months.

Lockheed Martin initiated a low-visibility program to develop a hydrogen tank for the X-33 made from the same aluminum-lithium alloy used in the latest lightweight space shuttle external tanks. VentureStar also abandoned its plans to use composite tanks and baselined aluminum-lithium tanks. NASA committed to fund the estimated $32 million that the new X-33 tanks would cost. In September 2000, Lockheed Martin and NASA agreed on the change to aluminum LH2 tanks for the X-33, and set a tentative launch date in mid-2003.

Reverting to aluminum tanks will also have a significant impact on performance. As early as May 1997, Skunk Works had recognized that the vehicle was going to be 5,000 to 6,000 pounds over its target weight, and that was when the composite tanks were still at the baseline weight. Although an ambitious weight-saving program had recovered much of the earlier 5,000 pounds, the latest vehicle is still overweight and will probably not be able to achieve much more than Mach 12, a significant decrement from the Mach 15 goal. The pressures and temperatures encountered at Mach 12 are not sufficient to completely validate the design. The current test program calls for the first five flights to land at Michael Army Air Field in Utah, and the next two flights will land at Malmstrom AFB. After this, there may be up to eight more test flights to improve the understanding of various aspects of vehicle and technology performance. The test objectives on these flights will be determined after the initial flights have been completed.

Work on the X-33 has continued at the Palmdale assembly facility during the tank investigation and subsequent negotiations between NASA and Lockheed Martin. By spring of 2001, the assembly of the X-33 flight vehicle was 75 percent complete, and more than 95 percent of the vehicle's components had been fabricated, tested, and delivered to Palmdale. NASA and Lockheed Martin are now proceeding with design of aluminum liquid hydrogen tanks for the X-33 to replace the experimental composite tanks that were originally planned.

The mid-2003 launch date is contingent on Lockheed Martin's ability to compete and win additional funding under the new NASA Space Launch Initiative (SLI). NASA and Lockheed believe it is critical to continue work, and the restructured plan focuses on providing milestone payments to Lockheed Martin's industry team for completed testing and delivery of their hardware and software systems. Additionally, the plan includes greater emphasis on mission safety and more ground demonstration of critical technology prior to actual flight. NASA is intent on ensuring that the lessons learned from other programs are taken into consideration in any go-forward planning. The X-33 required no additional funding from NASA through March 2001, but the project will need additional funding from the SLI for completion.

VentureStar Concept

The original baseline VentureStar configuration, dubbed L1, featured a delta-shaped planform, blunt forebody, and smooth upper and lower surface contours. The fineness ratio of the vehicle was optimized within the constraints of payload bay length and propellant volume requirements. Seven linear aerospike engines were integrated into the aft body tank closures and provided structure for the attachment of the stabilizers. A 45-foot-long, 15-foot-diameter payload bay cavity was nestled between the two LH2 tanks. Performance requirements developed by market analyses sized the LEO payload capacity at 43,000 pounds.

Originally, the VentureStar propellant tanks consisted of one composite multi-lobe main LO2 tank in the forward portion of the vehicle, and two composite multi-lobe main LH2 tanks that began at the LO2 tank closure and ended at the linear aerospike engines. These tanks also carried the primary structural loads. In addition to the main tanks, there were auxiliary tanks for the orbital maneuvering system located below the payload bay cavity forward of the aerospike engine. The main propellant system feed lines were routed internally between the payload bay cavity and the auxiliary tanks.

The cylindrical payload bay was located on the vehicle centerline over the vehicle landing center of gravity to provide minimal trim changes between payload in or out. The payload bay doors were integrated into the upper body surface, and because of the LH2 tank structure, did not have to carry structural loads. The payload bay walls were the large insulated LH2 tanks on either side, and the thrust and intertank structures were located on the end.

The primary subsystems bay was located forward in the intertank structure between the LO2 tank and the payload bay cavity. Operational considerations, such as accessibility to systems routinely checked between flights, were a critical element of the ongoing design process. Distributed subsystems were placed adjacent to openings that were required anyway, such as the payload cavity and the landing gear wells, to facilitate a minimum number of intrusions through the TPS for routine maintenance. The main landing gear was placed on a lobe of the LH2 tanks and retracted toward the vehicle centerline while the nose gear was located on the crease of the LO2 tank and retracted aft.

The large body radii and low planform loading afforded by the lifting-body shape was believed to result in lower re-entry heating than either a wing-body or a conical shape. This enabled the consideration of several lightweight material combinations for the primary structure and TPS. The result was the application of composite and metallic materials for primary structure and TPS, resulting in a robust, easily maintained system.

Body flaps extended from the lower surface of the vehicle outboard of the linear aerospike engine on each side. This was one of the most visible changes from the original design, which had body flaps extending from both the upper and lower surfaces. The flaps could be deflected to generate pitch, roll, and yaw moments for aerodynamic control and trim during descent. Canted vertical stabilizers were employed for aerodynamic stability and control. The leading edges of the stabilizers were swept aft to an angle inside the shock wave during atmospheric re-entry to minimize aerodynamic heating. Primary yaw authority is provided by ruddevators mounted on the tail surfaces.

The projected gross liftoff weight (GLOW) for VentureStar is 1,800,000 pounds with a 25,000-payload delivered to the ISS orbit. Nominal orbital insertion weight for the baseline ISS mission is approximately 220,000 pounds. Fluctuations in vehicle size and weight are anticipated during the design iteration process; however, the ratio of inserted weight (vehicle dry weight plus payload plus on-orbit fluids) to GLOW must remain below approximately 12 percent to achieve a successful SSTO. This requires that the vehicle dry mass fraction be maintained below 10 percent.

Although the VentureStar was originally baselined to use a composite liquid oxygen tank, Lockheed used a conventional aluminum-lithium 2195 alloy LO2 tank for the X-33, shown here being installed in the airframe. The X-33 was supposed to use composite liquid hydrogen tanks as a demonstration of this crucial technology required for VentureStar. This has proven the most difficult hurdle to overcome in the X-33 program, and the composite LH2 tanks have suffered a variety of setbacks until finally one of the LH2 tanks completely failed during structural testing in November 1999. *Lockheed Martin Skunk Works photo by Floyd Clark*

Another aspect of the X-33 program that is often overlooked is the advances in launch techniques it is supposed to demonstrate. Instead of the large, complex, and expensive launch sites used by the space shuttle and most other rockets, X-33 (and VentureStar) are supposed to use relatively small, austere launch complexes. This is an artist's concept of the X-33 complex at Haystack Butte on the edge of Edwards AFB. Other than some propellant tanks, a single movable hanger, and the launch mount, there is very little here. *Lockheed Martin Skunk Works drawing by John Frassanito & Associates, Inc.*

The Skunk Works design for VentureStar has evolved considerably during the 10 years it has been under consideration. Initially, the vehicle was a true lifting-body with interchangeable nose sections that could house a two-person cockpit for piloted missions, or advanced computers for autonomous missions. The cockpit was quickly dropped and an autonomous vehicle was baselined. Slowly the shape has evolved away from its lifting-body origins, based primarily on unfavorable wind tunnel results. It has been difficult to define a configuration that is acceptably stable during all phases of flight. At first the variations were minor; the underbody was made flatter, and then wider. Soon, small stabilizers were added to the sides of the aft body. These continued to grow until they began to look more like wings. The lower part of the aft body sprouted flaps, and forward canards were briefly toyed with to cure an instability in the transonic (Mach 0.9–2.0) range.

Early on in the design stage, it was decided to use an encapsulated payload concept where the payload would be enclosed in a standard-size capsule at the satellite manufacturer. This capsule would be placed into a large payload bay in the center of the lifting-body to eliminate the extensive reconfiguration required on the space shuttle between each mission. The payload bay was initially sized to be similar to the one on the shuttle—50 feet long by 15 feet square. The goal for VentureStar is to carry 56,000 pounds to LEO, 25,000 pounds to the ISS, and 18,000 pounds to geosynchronous transfer orbit (GTO). These capabilities are roughly equivalent to those of the space shuttle.

The difficulties that were encountered during the development of the X-33 composite propellant tanks have forced VentureStar to abandon them, at least for now. The new aluminum tanks could not fit in the same space allocated for the composite tanks, and eventually encroached on the area reserved for the payload bay. Initially, Skunk Works moved the payload up, partially outside the smooth mold line of the upper surface, which resulted in a semi-submerged payload. Skunk Works didn't want to compromise the payload capacity of the vehicle and eventually elected to move the payload outside into a pod carried on top of the main body. Although it is detrimental to the overall drag characteristics of the vehicle, this arrangement does offer some advantages. The most significant advantage is that payloads of virtually any size and shape can theoretically be carried. Adapting the external payload forced Skunk Works to move the vertical stabilizers, which had been located on top of the aft body, to the tips of even larger wings. This, in turn, caused the wings and their associated structures to be made stronger, increased the weight of the vehicle, and forced more propellants to be carried. It is a viscious cycle.

Thermal Protection

A trade study was conducted by Skunk Works to determine whether the lifting-body structure should be hot or cold. The X-15 is a good example of a hot structure, while the space shuttle orbiter exemplifies a cold structure. The principle driver was all-up weight, and candidate material categories varied from cool plastics to hot metals. Included were graphite-epoxy, Bismaleimide, Polyimide, titanium, stainless steel, and nickel steel. Preliminary analysis showed the ascent phase to be the design driver for the TPS, while the descent was relatively benign.

The results of the trade study concluded that a moderately warm (350 degrees Fahrenheit) graphite-composite primary airframe structure offered the lowest all-up weight. It was found that for structural temperatures above 350 degrees Fahrenheit, the TPS weight did not decrease enough to compensate for the increase in density of higher-heat-capacity materials. Further, it was found that a moderately warm composite structure was well within the capabilities to design and manufacture.

The re-entry trajectory selected for the RLV was specifically tailored to minimize the peak heat rate during re-entry. The lifting-body's low planform loading allows a cooler re-entry than the space shuttle, and the lower surface temperatures expected during re-entry allow the use of a well-characterized, conventional, and durable TPS. Oxidation-resistant carbon-carbon (ORCC) was selected for the highest temperature regions encountered such as the nose cap and leading edges because it provides superior oxidation resistance and has higher temperature capability as compared to Advanced Carbon-Carbon (ACC-4), Carbon-Silicone-Carbon (SC), and SiC-SiC materials.

For temperatures under 1,800 degrees Fahrenheit, Inconol-617 was selected for its high-temperature creep performance, thermomechanical, and chemical stability. For temperatures under 1,300 degrees Fahrenheit, Titanium-1100 was selected because it is a production-ready titanium alloy. For the comparatively low temperatures encountered on the leeward side of the vehicle, conventional insulation blankets consisting of PBI, AFRSI, and TABI were selected for use.

VentureStar Engines

VentureStar's main engine is a pump-fed linear aerospike engine that uses liquid hydrogen and liquid oxygen propellants. Unlike a typical bell nozzle, the aerospike nozzle opens to the atmosphere and allows for an automatic performance adjustment as the vehicle ascends. The truncated planar spike nozzle utilizes secondary flow to pressurize the nozzle base region, and thus compensates for the shortened length. The secondary flow is provided by the engine's turbine drive gas, which is exhausted into the base after it expands through the turbines. This serendipitous use of the turbine drive gases permits the simple generator cycle to match the performance of complex topping cycle engines.

The launch concept for VentureStar is not much different from the X-33, although it will require a slightly more complex launch site only because it has to deal with payloads and a larger vehicle. Unlike the shuttle where each payload requires the payload bay to be specially configured, VentureStar expects to use a containerized payload concept where the satellite (or other item) is installed in a standard container which is then loaded into the vehicle. The payload container is suspended in the hanger in the background. *Lockheed Martin Skunk Works drawing by John Frassanito & Associates, Inc.*

The high-pressure primary flow gases that produce the major portion of the engine thrust are exhausted from modular thrusters against the surface of an external expansion ramp. The primary flow continues to expand beyond the nozzle surface and encloses a subsonic, recirculating flow field in the base region. The pressure acting upon the nozzle base contributes additional thrust to the nozzle, and with the introduction of the secondary flow, further increases the base pressure.

The outer surface of the primary flow is a free jet boundary, which is influenced by ambient pressure. This ambient pressure favorably influences nozzle performance at low altitudes. At sea level, the relatively high ambient pressure compresses the primary flow field and increases the static pressure on the nozzle wall. At high altitudes, the outer free jet boundary expands to the Prandtl-Meyer turning angle at the exit of the modular thruster. The ambient pressure influence prevents the nozzle from overexpanding at sea level and allows the use of high area ratio nozzles for high vacuum specific impulse.

The linear aerospike engine uses a unique thrust vector control (TVC) scheme where differential thrust control is accomplished by adjusting the propellant flows between the upper and lower engine segment thrust cells. This provides both pitch and roll control through the use of electromechanical actuated three-way showerhead valves. Vehicle yaw control is accomplished by varying the output of individual turbo pumps and engine thrust. This simple control architecture eliminates the necessity for gimbals, actuators, hydraulic plumbing, and the increased power required to move the engines for TVC. The aerospike engine can be closely coupled to the aft end of the vehicle to shorten the thrust structure without the attendant gimbals joints, thus effectively moving the center of gravity forward and driving the vehicle empty weight down.

Initially, when the X-33 was scheduled to fly in March 1999, Lockheed Martin believed VentureStar could make its first flight as early as 2003. As development of the X-33 has lagged, the flight date for VentureStar has slipped, first to 2004, and now indefinitely. There have also been other difficulties for Lockheed Martin. The corporation as a whole has been badly impacted by its rash of acquisitions during the 1990s that contributed to the rapid growth of the company. These created significant management challenges that have resulted in numerous changes in corporate goals, and the general realignment of business units that saw Skunk Works absorbed into the newly created Aeronautics Company.

The trouble, real or perceived, of the corporation as a whole has had a detrimental effect on VentureStar. Unlike every major launch vehicle that has preceded it,

Stop the Presses!

NASA announced on March 1, 2001, that it would not add Space Launch Initiative (SLI) funds to the X-33 program. As a result, the X-33 program was effectively cancelled when the cooperative agreement between NASA and Lockheed Martin expired on March 31, 2001. NASA was quick to point out that Lockheed Martin could choose to go forward with the program and use its own funds, but the aerospace giant decided against the investment and began moves to shut the program down. The VentureStar™ program was closed down at the same time.

The continuation of X-33 had depended upon successfully competing for Space Launch Initiative funding under a NASA Research Announcement that will lead to award of some $900 million over the next two-and-a-half years. That solicitation was issued in October 2000, and industry proposals were submitted in December 2000. Contract awards could be awarded as early as April, but none of those negotiations will include X-33 or X-34. NASA determined that the benefits to be derived from flight testing these X-vehicles did not warrant the magnitude of government investment required, and that SLI funds should be applied to higher priority needs.

More than 300 personnel from throughout NASA participated in the SLI proposal evaluation process. "This has been a very tough decision but we think it is the right business decision," said Art Stephenson, director of NASA's Marshall Space Flight Center in Huntsville, Alabama. Marshall manages the SLI, X-33, and X-34 programs for NASA. "We have gained a tremendous amount of knowledge from these X-programs, but one of the things we have learned is that our technology has not yet advanced to the point that we can successfully develop a new reusable launch vehicle that substantially improves safety, reliability, and affordability."

"The Space Launch Initiative will take us to that point. It is a comprehensive, long-range plan to promote commercial development and civil exploration of space, and provides the strategy and funding to enable at least two competing architectures for full-scale development of a second-generation reusable launch vehicle by mid-decade," added Stephenson. "Through focused risk-reduction activities and risk-reduction technology development, we will make significant improvements in safety, reliability, and affordability over the launch capability we have today. A new launch system that meets these goals could begin operating early in the next decade."

The NASA investment in the X-33 program totaled $912 million and stayed within its 1996 budget projection for the program. Lockheed Martin and its industry partners originally committed to invest $212 million in the X-33, and during the life of the program, the amount increased to $357 million. As of the end of March 2001, the X-33 vehicle was 75 percent complete, with over 95 percent of the hardware having been delivered. The major outstanding item was a set of aluminum LH2 tanks. The launch site at Haystack Butte was also complete, and most modifications to range systems needed to support the flight test program had been completed.

Lockheed Martin has been attempting to interest the Air Force into continuing the X-33 program, as well as funding a follow-on X-33B that would allow a limited orbital capability. As of April 2001, the military has been unable to commit to the program due to an uncertain budgetary outlook. Once the new Bush administration has defined military priorities, the Air Force might be willing to fund the program. For the time being Lockheed has arranged to keep the mostly-built X-33 vehicle in storage in its assembly jig in Palmdale. Most of the engineers and other personnel have been reassigned to other programs within their corporations, so the Skunk Works' first spaceship will have to wait.

VentureStar is a true commercial enterprise. Other than the NASA participation in the X-33 project, VentureStar is being funded entirely through venture capital. Wall Street has been reluctant to commit major funding to VentureStar based partially on its views of Lockheed Martin's current struggles. Combined with the failure of the largest venture-capital space business to date—Iridium—it is very unlikely that VentureStar will find significant funding in the near future. Still, Lockheed believes in VentureStar, and on January 26, 1999, created the VentureStar Limited Liability Company (LLC) to "identify potential strategic partners and obtain all necessary commitments to meet established financial goals and key program milestones." Only time will tell.

Six

Like many other C-130s, the COMBAT TALON special ops aircraft have been modified with the UARRSI aerial refueling receptacle on top of the fuselage. This allows the aircraft to be refueled from KC-135 or KC-10 tankers using the standard flying boom technique instead of the probe-and-drogue technique used by most other C-130s. This COMBAT TALON is carrying a pair of ECM pods on the outer wing pylons and shows the variety of bumps and bulges required by antennas for its various systems. *Lockheed Martin Skunk Works*

>> Skunk Works Today–
ENGINEERING SERVICES

Core Strengths

Although Skunk Works is primarily known to the public as the manufacturer of top-secret spy aircraft, it has always undertaken other projects as well. On occasion, these projects, such as the Sea Shadow stealth ship, are not even related to aircraft; other times they are only related on the periphery.

For instance, Skunk Works recently participated in the study and development of Systems Requirements and Mission Analysis simulation tools to help evolve mission operational concepts, define and verify system requirements, and quantify system survivability and effectiveness. One of the key contributions from Skunk Works to this ongoing work was to tailor these models to evaluate low-observable technologies, and to compare the results with real combat conditions such as Desert Storm and Kosovo. These tools allow mission analysts to quickly reach a preliminary answer for design guidance, or to conduct detailed performance assessments.

In a related field, Skunk Works has developed a systems engineering approach that ensures design tradeoffs are carefully analyzed and traceable, and avoids the burden of an overly rigid process. This is particularly important since the application of new technology to highly complex weapons and the requirement that systems be seamlessly integrated into existing force structures requires a disciplined systems engineering approach in order to meet design and cost realities. Skunk Works maintains an outstanding reputation in LO technology. Specially-developed, LO design and development tools provide capabilities that include concept development, design, fabrication, test, and evaluation, as well as a signature measurement of vehicles, antennas, and coatings. LO evaluations are provided at a dedicated

Sea Shadow

Probably the most radical departure from Skunk Works' normal projects (if any Skunk Works project can be called normal) is the *Sea Shadow*. This highly-unusual ship was developed under a program conducted by the Defense Advanced Research Projects Agency (DARPA), the Navy, and Lockheed Martin Missiles and Space Company, with significant participation by Skunk Works. The *Sea Shadow* program began in the mid-1980s to explore a variety of new technologies for surface ships, including ship control, structures, automation for reduced manning, seakeeping, and LO technologies. The Sea Shadow was assembled in complete secrecy. Parts from different manufacturers were brought to Redwood City, California, and assembled inside a large former mining barge. The ship was finally revealed to the public in 1993 and underwent daylight testing. A year later, the *Sea Shadow* was retired and stored inside its barge in San Diego. The original *Sea Shadow* test program influenced the design of the Navy's *Arleigh Burke*-, and T-AGOS-class ships.

In anticipation of conducting future ship research and development testing, the navy and the Lockheed Martin Advanced Technologies Laboratory (ATL) began to reactivate the *Sea Shadow* in January 1999. In a rush to have the ship ready to participate in the San Francisco Bay experiments, the Lockheed Martin companies collaborated to make the ship seaworthy, repair its dry dock barge, and train a crew in just nine weeks. The shipyard repairs were performed by the National Steel and Shipbuilding Company. The *Sea Shadow's* return to service began with a flourish at the Navy's Fleet Battle Experiment Echo in March where the ship played the role of an adversary by supporting Special Warfare teams and simulating missile attacks against navy vessels. The exercise in San Francisco Bay also provided ATL with an opportunity to demonstrate several prototype systems aimed at reducing crew size and improving ship survivability.

The *Sea Shadow* will support risk reduction for future surface ship platforms such as the navy's twenty-first century Land Attack Destroyer (DD-21), recently named the *Zumwalt* class. The platform will allow the Navy to explore and test, in a realistic at-sea environment, important DD-21 advanced information and automation technologies that support reduced manning, and ship survivability. Notable demonstrations will include DARPA's High-Performance Distributed Computing experiment and artificial-intelligence technologies for combat systems and ship control. ATL has been involved with the *Sea Shadow* since 1993. The *Sea Shadow* is an efficient test platform because it can be modified quickly and operated cost-effectively. As a test ship with significant onboard automation, the *Sea Shadow* can be operated around the clock with an eight-member crew. A much larger crew would be needed to operate a commissioned navy ship of comparable size.

Sponsored by the Naval Sea Systems Command, the *Sea Shadow* is 164 feet long, is 68 feet at maximum beam, displaces 560 tons, and draws 14.5 feet. It can reach a maximum speed of 14 knots by using diesel electric propulsion.

There is very little deck space aboard the *Sea Shadow*, primarily because there is no deck. Therefore, most operations are conducted very much like those on a submarine. One report in the popular press indicated that the *Sea Shadow* was so stealthy that it passed within a few thousand yards of a navy cruiser that was specifically looking for it without being observed. Whether this is true will probably never be known for sure, but the *Sea Shadow* has had an effect on how the world's navies design ships. *Lockheed Martin Skunk Works*

After a long period in storage, the *Sea Shadow* was reactivated in January 1999 to support developing technologies for the next generation of U.S. Navy destroyers; the DD-21, since named the *Zumwalt* class. Skunk Works has not been directly involved in the *Sea Shadow's* new lease on life, but it is undoubtedly providing support as needed to the Lockheed Martin Advanced Technology Laboratories, which is conducting the tests. *Lockheed Martin Skunk Works*

test facility that is continuously updated to redefine the state-of-the-art static and flight testing of airframes. Avionics provides a complete definition of vehicle and subsystem performance.

The aerodynamic, thermodynamic, propulsion, and stability-and-control challenges posed by aircraft like the F-117A and DarkStar are substantial, and Skunk Works maintains a staff of specialists in these areas. Complete physical and virtual modeling capabilities are part of a unique approach to analyzing and optimizing flight and mission performance. Skunk Works also has extensive experience with integrating advanced avionics systems architectures and processors for real-time airborne signal and data processing in constantly changing threat and mission environments. Unique Skunk Works avionics capabilities include LO apertures and radomes, advanced sensor integration, wideband satellite communications, smart skins, and automated mission planning. Expertise in advanced structures is constantly being used to develop new methods for analyzing loads, stress, flutter, and dynamics, as well as finite element modeling and computational fluid dynamics. New materials and processes, including a wide range of composites, are continually being developed by Skunk Works, and are particularly applicable to LO technologies.

Continuing the original tradition of Skunk Works, sophisticated 3-D design tools are integrated with simulation and manufacturing to support a complete manufacturing capability from tool design through prototyping or limited production. Many of the specialized manufacturing processes used in Palmdale are unique to Skunk Works. Support, production, and quality are critical issues for most Skunk Works customers, and the ability to arrive at an elegant, cost-effective engineering solution requires a fundamental approach to design that emphasizes the engineer's awareness and understanding of the requirements of a wide range of disciplines, and the implications of new technologies, including computer-based design.

The current Skunk Works encompasses six basic lines of business: Tactical Systems, Reconnaissance Systems, Reusable Launch Vehicles, Advanced Programs, Modification Programs, and various BIG SAFARI programs. The highly classified nature of many Skunk Works activities prohibits the disclosure of certain technologies and projects currently being developed, but some are nevertheless well known.

Tactical Systems

The F-117A is the only operational, combat proven, LO weapon system currently in the air force inventory. Building on its unique capabilities (as dramatically demonstrated in the Gulf War), the F-117A continues to be enhanced through upgrades in avionics, observables, navigation systems, and sensor technologies. It is expected to remain in front-line service until the year 2030. The F-22 Raptor capitalizes on the expertise honed through the development of HAVE BLUE and the F-117A in part through Skunk Works' contributions in affordable, LO radome technology, materials development/production, and vehicle/component low-observables testing. The Lockheed Martin Joint Strike Fighter (JSF) began at Skunk Works, and as part of a Lockheed Martin team, Skunk Works is designing, building, and flight-testing the two X-35 JSF concept demonstration aircraft.

Reconnaissance Systems

A variety of upgrades and improvements of the U-2 have allowed it to remain the premier tactical reconnaissance aircraft for almost 40 years. Now equipped with more fuel-efficient General Electric F118 engines, the U-2's new system configuration represents a highly integrated, multi-sensor airborne and ground system that maximizes real-time production and dissemination of data to the war fighter. The U-2 fleet operates worldwide missions on a daily basis, and Skunk Works is involved in every sortie. The air force expects to keep the U-2 in service through the year 2020.

Top: Skunk Works was called upon by Lockheed Martin's Electronics & Missiles Division (now Lockheed Martin Integrated Systems—LMIS) to manufacture nine test vehicles for the JASSM competition, which Lockheed Martin subsequently won. Production missiles will be manufactured by LMIS at a new Pike County Operations facility in Troy, Alabama. This stealthy cruise missile will be used by a variety of air force, navy, and marine platforms, including the F-16 and F/A-18. In this photo the missile's wings have not deployed from their location along the bottom of the fuselage, and the flight data probe is nonstandard. *Lockheed Martin Skunk Works photo by Tom Reynolds*

Lower: This is the current home of Skunk Works in Palmdale. The facility had originally been built to manufacture Lockheed L-1011 TriStar airliners, and sat mostly unused after that program was completed. When Skunk Works arrived at the location, a few new buildings were added and security was significantly tightened. This is the main gate to the facility (located at 1011 Lockheed Way), and five of the aircraft on display can be seen—an A-12, U-2D, F-104G, and on poles in the background, an F-80 and F-117. *Lockheed Martin Skunk Works*

DarkStar embodied the latest technology in airborne reconnaissance, and incorporated a LO design with advanced stealth features. It could fly above 45,000 feet, had more than a 500-nautical-mile operating radius, and its mission duration was in excess of eight hours. Unfortunately, the program was canceled in February 1999 due to budgetary constraints.

Reusable Launch Vehicles

Lockheed Martin is leading Phase II of the X-33 program that is valued at more than $1 billion through the year 2001. This may be followed by the development of a full-scale operational VentureStar reusable launch vehicle as a commercial venture. By making access to space more affordable, Skunk Works will pave the way for future entrepreneurs to develop new products, services, companies, jobs, and industries in much the same manner that trains, automobiles, and airplanes created vast new opportunities for American commerce.

Winning the X-33 contract involved close teamwork between four of Lockheed Martin's six primary business sectors, plus support from key industry partners. The effort was led by Skunk Works and others in the aeronautics sector, and joined by operating companies from the space and strategic missiles sector, information & technology services sector, and electronics sector.

Advanced Programs

Skunk Works combined with other Lockheed Martin divisions to bid on the AGM-158 Joint Air-to-Surface Standoff Missile (JASSM), a long-range (100+ nautical miles) strike weapon. During the early program definition and risk reduction (PDRR) phase, Skunk Works designed and fabricated nine test vehicles for Lockheed Martin's Electronics & Missiles Division (now Lockheed Martin Integrated Systems—LMIS), the prime system integrator. Lockheed Martin won the JASSM competition, and production missiles will be manufactured by LMIS at the new Pike County Operations facility in Troy, Alabama. The program is currently toward the end of a 40-month engineering and manufacturing development (EMD) phase, and production began in January 2001.

One of the Department of Defense's highest priority programs, JASSM is designed to provide a long-range standoff capability against a wide array of high-value, heavily defended targets. Its GPS navigation system, state-of-the-art infrared seeker, 1,000-pound precursor warhead, and stealth airframe make it virtually impossible to defend against. Pilots will be able to launch the deadly missile from well outside the range of enemy air defenses, and it will cruise autonomously in virtually any weather, day or night, to its target with pinpoint accuracy. The 2,250-pound, 14-foot-long missile is designed to be launched from the B-1, B-2, B-52, F-16, and F/A-18. The missile has been test fitted to the F-117A, but there are no current plans for the stealth fighter to use it. "We're very pleased to move forward into the heart of this important development effort," said Dick Caime, Lockheed Martin's vice president of strike weapon systems. "I'm confident that the same talented industry/customer team that got us this far will deliver the first production model of this extraordinary weapon on schedule."

Another example of an advanced program at Skunk Works is the Technologies for Reliable Autonomous Control (TRAC). The two primary objectives of this program are to develop a novel representation of an air vehicle's information state that can uniquely encode all control and operational mode invariants and will enable changes in the air vehicle's system state and health to be autonomously identified with high precision; and make use of the active state model to develop vehicle health management capabilities such as autonomous real-time fault prognosis/diagnosis, autonomous error recover, and residual life assessment algorithms that can be used for condition-based air vehicle maintenance. The development of these technologies will help mitigate some of the existing flaws in autonomous air vehicles including

unacceptable failure rates and control challenges such as tight response envelope requirements.

To accomplish these tasks, Skunk Works is developing the next generation of capabilities for air vehicle control and management based upon a new "control adaptation" and "high-frequency control switching" algorithmic framework. This includes the development of an in-line, time-dependant expansion of an active state estimate with infinite local stability and terminal convergence properties to provide increased control robustness in a poorly modeled and changing flight environment. The program is also conducting a theoretical analysis of the machine representation and interpretation of the air vehicle's internal state (health), intent (mission), operating context (environment), and contact interface (controllability) that can be used to maintain, switch, and mix control modes.

The end product of this research will be the development of a formal model that can support non-monotonic spatio-temporal (forward and backward in time) transitions to enable predictive assessment and post-inferencing. This approach will couple notions of information uncertainty with a nonlinear model, nonlinear control formalisms, and adaptations. This will validate new capabilities for system fault diagnosis and prognosis using an active state model instead of reacting to events as they occur. The formal model will then be used to demonstrate active state model-based technologies by applying them (in simulation) to UAV control issues including situational awareness, collision avoidance, and system failures.

Modification Programs

Beginning in 1956, Lockheed Aircraft Services (LAS) in Ontario, California, began performing a wide variety of specialized modification programs for the military services, foreign governments, and commercial operators. These modifications included special airborne platforms for electronic warfare and command, control

For 40 years beginning in 1956, Lockheed Aircraft Services (LAS) has modified a wide variety of aircraft at this facility in Ontario, California. Several C-130s and a single L-1011 can be seen in this photo, along with a good number of A-4 Skyhawks. The two C-130s in the foreground are being modified to the COMPASS CALL configuration. The entire LAS operation was moved to Palmdale and merged with Skunk Works in June 1996. *Lockheed Martin Skunk Works*

One of the projects conducted by LAS, and later by Skunk Works, was the modernization of McDonnell Douglas A-4 Skyhawks. Here is an A-4AR FightingHawk destined for the Argentine Air Force. The first five FightingHawks were turned over in Palmdale on December 17, 1997, as part of a three-year, $200-million contract to modify 36 ex-Marine A-4s (32 A-4Ms and 4 OA-4Ms) to the A-4AR configuration. *Lockheed Martin Skunk Works photo by Denny Lombard*

and communications assignments, installing a sophisticated airborne telescope for NASA, and modifying nine C-130 Hercules into fully equipped, completely self-contained hospital aircraft. In the past 45 years, LAS has modified or upgraded nearly 200,000 aircraft from Boeing, Douglas, Hughes, Lockheed, and other domestic and foreign manufacturers.

In June 1996, Lockheed Martin Aircraft Services was consolidated with Skunk Works in Palmdale. Aircraft Services became a business line within Skunk Works, and the transfer of programs and personnel to Palmdale began immediately. The October 1996 arrival of an EC-130H COMPASS CALL electronic warfare aircraft marked the beginning of a transition of BIG SAFARI work from Ontario to Palmdale. The aircraft was delivered back at Davis-Monthan AFB in Arizona during December 1997. The Ontario facility was closed in late 1998, and all operations are now conducted at the Skunk Works facility in Palmdale.

Skunk Works Aircraft Services has exceptional manufacturing capabilities in composites, sheet metal, electrical/electronic, and machining operations. Complete technical field services are available worldwide, and for over 45 years, Lockheed has supported aircraft around the globe. Aircraft Services has the engineering and technical experts to make repairs, installations, and modifications, as well as provide every level of maintenance, anywhere in the world.

Aircraft Services also specializes in the design, system integration, fabrication, and installation of hardware and software systems for special mission aircraft. Additional services include systems management, depot-level aircraft maintenance, and total logistics support. Among these services is a "quick response capability" designed to deliver modified aircraft quickly in response to an emergency situation. A recent example of this capability was the response to the downing of an Italian G-222 transport aircraft on a humanitarian mission in Bosnia. Three months later, Skunk Works Aircraft Services delivered three LIGHTNING BOLT C-130s upgraded with new infrared missile self-protection systems that were deployed instead of the G-222s, which lacked any kind of warning system.

Other noteworthy modification programs include installing the UARRSI (Universal Aerial Refueling Receptacle Slipway Installation) on over 100 C-130s. With long endurance at a premium for special operations, jamming, and intelligence gathering, BIG SAFARI first decided to install the modified KC-135 in-flight refueling system (renamed the UARRSI) on C-130s in 1976, and Lockheed had the first modified aircraft flying within six months. In an early demonstration, 17 Navy SEALs were carried nonstop across the Pacific Ocean on a 27.75-hour flight to make a nighttime, over-water air drop in the Philippines. Aircraft Services also excels in the design and manufacture of aircraft systems trainers. To date, more than 1,000 systems trainers have been delivered to government and private customers worldwide, including systems for the C-5 Galaxy, Canada's CP-140 Aurora (P-3) antisubmarine warfare aircraft, AH-64 Apache attack helicopter, and the F-117A stealth fighter.

Big Safari Programs

BIG SAFARI is the Air Force program office responsible for the sustainment and modification of specialized special mission aircraft. BIG SAFARI is not a technology project per se, but is a specialized process of acquisition and contract management that supports 20 to 24 projects at any one time and includes logistics responsibility for over 50 aircraft. This process was the basis for the LIGHTNING BOLT initiatives and is used to accomplish special projects on a quick-reaction basis. Although the BIG SAFARI process has always operated at minimum funding levels due to the effectiveness of its management procedures and is far more streamlined than any other program due to the nature of its authority, the recent Defense Acquisition Reform Initiatives have helped realize a larger cost savings. BIG SAFARI was also employed to support the 1994 reactivation of the SR-71, and it was the only Air Force office that tried to promote the program. Over the years, Lockheed has supported BIG SAFARI with a variety of modification projects, mainly to C-130 aircraft.

BIG SAFARI became a permanent fixture at LAS in 1964 with the establishment of an office (Detachment 4) in Ontario specifically to oversee modification of aircraft for special missions in Southeast Asia. The first task was the DUCK HOOK modification of six C-123Bs with special ECM receivers and transmitters, Doppler navigation systems, and camouflage paint. These were first-generation deep-penetration jamming aircraft that operated for most of the war in Southeast Asia. The aircraft were eventually retired in 1971, and most were probably transferred to South Korea or Taiwan.

MC-130 Rivet Yard/Combat Talon

Another project that began in 1964 was the modification of several C-130s to support the classified HEAVY CHAIN covert, low-level supply missions. These aircraft were equipped with surveillance equipment, terrain-following radar, and a sophisticated ECM self-protection suite. The first effort was code-named OUT YONDER and subsequently evolved into RIVET YARD that added special fuel-tank baffling to limit damage from anti aircraft fire, a high-speed, low-level aerial delivery

Improved systems have resulted in the COMBAT TALON II aircraft shown here. The most obvious addition is the white GPS antenna over the fuselage, but many other changes have been incorporated as well. A pair of ECM pods is carried on the outer wing pylons, and the FLIR turret can be seen under the nose. COMBAT TALON aircraft can be used to distribute psychological warfare leaflets, drop 20,000-pound BLU-82 fuel-air bombs to detonate minefields, serve as pathfinders, and operate as en route tankers for search and rescue and reconnaissance missions. *Lockheed Martin Skunk Works*

system, and a forward-looking infrared (FLIR) system. HEAVY CHAIN missions were terminated in 1972, and the RIVET YARD aircraft were subsequently modified to COMBAT TALON standards.

COMBAT TALON MC-130s provided covert insertion, extraction, and support of special forces in Iraq and Kuwait during Operation Desert Storm. The aircraft also distributed psychological warfare leaflets, dropped 20,000-pound BLU-82 fuel-air bombs to detonate minefields, served as pathfinders, and operated as en route tankers for search and rescue and reconnaissance missions. Before the ground war started, the aircraft used sophisticated infrared equipment to record the infrared signatures of Iraqi tanks. This data was used for target

identification once combat operations began. COMBAT TALON also flew special terrain-following missions to fine-tune radar polarization, and improve the reception and processing of radar returns weakened by their reflection from sand, a concern in low-level desert operations.

C-130E STRAY GOOSE

During 1966 Project STRAY GOOSE installed the Fulton Recovery System on eight C-130E COMBAT KNIFE aircraft assigned to special operations units. This system allowed the modified aircraft to pick up people from the ground while flying extremely low and slow. It was a wild ride for the people being retrieved, and the system proved to be very successful. Three of the aircraft were eventually destroyed, including one that crashed deep in North Vietnam and another that was destroyed on the ground in Da Nang during a mortar attack.

EC-130E ABCCC

The seven EC-130E Airborne Battlefield Command and Control Center (ABCCC) aircraft have been modified by LAS to carry the USC-48 Airborne Battlefield Command and Control Center Capsules (ABCCC III) in their cargo compartments. The ABCCC aircraft have distinctive air conditioner heat exchangers in front of the engines, two HF radio antennas on both wingtips, three mushroom-shaped antennas on the top of the aircraft, numerous antennas under the fuselage, an UARRSI aerial refueling system, and special mounted rails for installing the USC-48 capsule.

Assigned to the Air Combat Command, the EC-130E ABCCC is an integral part of the air force's Tactical Air Control System. While functioning as a direct extension of ground-based command and control authorities, the primary mission is to provide flexibility in the overall control of tactical air resources. In order to accomplish this, the ABCCC can provide communications to higher headquarters, including national command authorities, under almost all peacetime and combat conditions.

Left and above: The Fulton Recovery System was first installed on C-130s during 1966 as part of Project STRAY GOOSE. This system allows a slow-moving, low-flying C-130 to snag a cable held aloft by a small balloon and retrieve whatever is on the other end of the cable. This can include small packages or people. The process is simple. The balloon holds the cable vertical, the C-130 snags it with the pinchers on the nose, and whatever is on the other ends snaps up to the open cargo ramp at the back of the aircraft where it is grabbed by waiting (and well-tethered) crewmen. Similar techniques have been used to retrieve space capsules (primarily carrying film from the original spy satellites) and other airborne objects. The system works surprisingly well, and a few modified C-130s are always waiting for assignments. *Lockheed Martin Skunk Works*

The USC-48 ABCCC III capsule is 40 feet long, weighs approximately 20,000 pounds, and costs $9 million. The ABCCC is an automated airborne command and control facility featuring computer-generated color displays, digitally controlled communications, and rapid data retrieval. The platform's 23 fully securable radios, secure teletype, and 15 computerized control consoles allow the battle staff to quickly analyze current combat situations and direct offensive air support under combat conditions. A recent upgrade equipped all seven ABC-CCs with the Joint Tactical Information Distribution System that allows real-time exchange of airborne tracks to through data links with Boeing E-3 Sentry AWACS aircraft. Mission roles include airborne extensions of the Air Operations Center (AOC) and Airborne Air Support Operations Center (ASOC) for command and control of Offensive Air Support (OAS) operations, and airborne on-scene command for special operations such as airdrops or evacuations.

EC-130E/J Commando Solo/Rivet Rider

Information warfare got its start with the CORONET SOLO, VOLANT SOLO, and RIVET RIDER projects in 1967.

The RIVET RIDER variant of the COMMANDO SOLO EC-130 includes VHF and UHF jamming capabilities, worldwide-format color TV, infrared countermeasures (chaff/flare dispensers plus infrared jammers), and self-contained INS/GPS navigation systems. In addition, a second wire antenna has been added that extends from under the fuselage and is held vertical by a 500-pound weight. RIVET RIDER also added a pair of 23-by-6-foot equipment pods under the wings and large X-shaped antennas mounted on both sides of the vertical stabilizer. *Lockheed Martin Skunk Works*

Four EC-121 Warning Stars (Super Constellations) were modified into EC-121S psychological warfare and stand-off jamming aircraft as part of CORONET SOLO. These aircraft were equipped to operate in the HF/MF radio and VHF and UHF television frequencies, and were flown by the 193rd Tactical Electronic Warfare Group of the Pennsylvania Air National Guard.

The equipment was cross-decked to C-130E aircraft in 1978. As part of VOLANT SOLO, the aircraft were updated in 1990 to allow transmission of both radio and television in a format compatible with the broadcast systems used in the Middle East in support of Operation Desert Shield. The aircraft were initially used to bolster Kuwaiti morale with the message that the Allies were coming. After combat began, the crews broadcast surrender appeals, Voice of America programs, and psychological messages aimed

at Iraqi tank crews. Further modifications resulted in the current COMMANDO SOLO configuration. Recently the equipment has begun to be cross-decked to new C-130J aircraft.

The EC-130 COMMANDO SOLO aircraft exist in COMFY LEVI and RIVET RIDER versions. COMFY LEVI conducts psychological operations and civil affairs broadcast missions in the standard AM, FM, HF, TV, and military communications bands. One oversized blade antenna is located under each wing, and a third extends forward from the vertical stabilizer. A retractable wire antenna is carried in a modified beaver tail and extends horizontally behind the aircraft. A typical mission consists of a single-ship orbit which is offset from the desired target audience and flies at the maximum altitudes possible to ensure optimum propagation patterns. Secondary missions include command and control communications countermeasures (C3CM) and limited intelligence gathering.

In addition to the basic COMFY LEVI equipment, RIVET RIDER modifications include VHF and UHF jamming capabilities, worldwide-format color TV, infrared countermeasures (chaff/flare dispensers plus infrared jammers), fire suppressant foam in the fuel tanks, radar warning receivers, and self-contained INS/GPS navigation systems. In addition, a second wire antenna has been added that extends vertically from under the fuselage and is held vertical by a 500-pound weight. RIVET RIDER also added a pair of 23-by-6-foot equipment pods under the wings and large X-shaped antennas mounted on both sides of the vertical stabilizer. Aircraft Services has modified six aircraft to the RIVET RIDER configuration.

Both COMMANDO SOLO versions have an unrefueled range of over 2,800 nautical miles, and are equipped with the UARRSI aerial refueling system in order to extend the broadcast time available on each mission.

EC-130H Compass Call/Rivet Fire

In 1977, Lockheed and Sanders Associates (now part of BAE Systems) were asked to develop a C-130-

The COMPASS CALL EC-130H is a highly capable jamming platform that was used extensively during the Gulf War to intercept and jam various Iraqi communication networks. The jammers require a large volume of cooling air. Notice the large intake on the left landing gear fairing on the EC-103H on the ground. A large array of wire antennas is suspended between the vertical and horizontal stabilizers, also evident in the ground shot. *Lockheed Martin Skunk Works photo by Denny Lombard*

based communications countermeasures system to jam critical command and control links with electronic noise. The eventual configuration added to the C-130Hs included computers, exciters, power amplifiers, and large external YAGI-type antennas. Initially the program was called COMPASS WIDGET, and Air Services modified the first two prototypes in less than 36 months. The program was renamed RIVET FIRE and evolved into an integrated communications jamming system. In 1980 BIG SAFARI authorized Aircraft Services to modify 16 additional aircraft as part of Project COMPASS CALL.

The goal of COMPASS CALL was to further integrate the jamming systems into a highly automated system capable of dealing with all known threats. This single

24-month project forced Aircraft Services to become involved in computers and software like no previous aircraft modification had. By all accounts, the modifications proved extremely successful. During Operation Desert Storm, COMPASS CALL EC-130Hs intercepted communications from Iraqi aircraft spotters reporting incoming strike aircraft, and successfully jammed them, essentially shutting down the Iraqi early warning system. COMPASS CALL also performed psychological operations and deception missions where the crews used their transmitters to taunt Iraqi radio operators and harass them with heavy metal music. When Iraqis began to associate COMPASS CALL jamming with upcoming strikes, Air Force crews began staging jamming in one area while strikes were carried out elsewhere.

COMPASS CALL is crucial in determining the enemy's electronic order of battle. In combination with COMMAND SOLO and classified space programs, COMPASS CALL denies the enemy use of his command and control systems. The EC-130H COMPASS CALL aircraft are the only wide-area offensive information warfare platform available to U.S. forces. COMPASS CALL provides a nonlethal means of denying and disrupting enemy command and control, degrading the combat capability, and reducing losses to friendly forces. COMPASS CALL primarily supports tactical air operations but also can provide jamming support to ground force operations.

Modifications to the aircraft include the addition of a RIVET FIRE ECM system, an UARRSI aerial refueling system, and advanced navigation and communications systems. The EC-130H carries a combat crew of 13 people—4 crew members are responsible for aircraft flight and navigation, while the other 9 crew members operate and maintain the RIVET FIRE equipment. The mission crew consists of an electronic warfare officer, an experienced cryptologic linguist, 6 analysis operators, and an airborne maintenance technician. Aided by the highly automated system developed by Aircraft Services, the mission crew analyzes the signal environment, designates targets, and ensures the system is operating effectively. Targets can be designated before the mission takes off, acquired in flight or through additional real-time tasking from outside agencies (i.e., AWACS commanders, RC-135).

The EC-130H COMPASS CALL fleet is currently being upgraded to a Block 30 configuration to improve system reliability and expand its capability against modern threats. These modifications totally rearrange the equipment on the EC-130H, and the primary architectural change is the elimination of the earlier single mainframe computer and the installation of a distributed system of workstations linked together by the largest fiber-optic network yet installed on an airborne platform.

The conversion to the Block 30 system, designed by Lockheed and several other contractors, has been a time-consuming project. Each aircraft requires approximately 16 months for modification at Skunk Works. Unlike other weapons systems which are tested before they are bought, Block 30 was purchased before being tested. All new hardware and a fivefold increase in the amount of software, which includes over one million lines of computer code, have produced the usual minor bugs that always seem to appear with new technology improvements. One common problem is the failure of a built-in self-test system, but Skunk Works and crews from the 41st Electronic Combat Squadron are working through the issues successfully. A proposed Block 35 initiative will inject new technology to further improve reliability and increase the Offensive Counter-Information (OCI) capability against modern command and control systems. However, a two-year funding gap exists between the completion of the first squadron and the start of modifications on the second squadron. This gap, and other funding reductions, have forced the Air Force to stretch out Block 30 completion to FY04, causing both fiscal inefficiencies and raising concerns of technical obsolescence in the equipment chosen for the modification.

Index

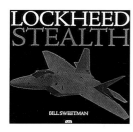